THE GREAT
WHITE FAIR

IRELAND IN OLD PHOTOGRAPHS

THE GREAT WHITE FAIR

THE HERBERT PARK EXHIBITION OF 1907

BRIAN SIGGINS

First published 2007
Reprinted 2011

The History Press Ireland
119 Lower Baggot Street
Dublin 2, Ireland
www.thehistorypress.ie

© Brian Siggins, 2007

The right of Brian Siggins to be identified as the Author
of this work has been asserted in accordance with the
Copyrights, Designs and Patents Act 1988.

British Library Cataloguing in Publication Data.
A catalogue record for this book is available from the British Library.

ISBN 978 1 84588 580 9

Typesetting and origination by The History Press
Printed in Great Britain
Manufacturing managed by Jellyfish Print Solutions Ltd

Contents

Introduction

My earliest memory of Herbert Park is of a winter's day some time before the Second World War. The pond had frozen over and was being skated on by men and women who were obviously working in the nearby continental embassies. They showed off skills which made us Dublin children envious. Since then the park has always held happy memories for me, and as my own children grew up, they too came to enjoy its delights. My grandchildren now spend many happy hours in a wonderful amenity.

My father had told me about a great exhibition held on the site of the park, but it wasn't until many years later, browsing in Kenny's Bookshop in Galway, that I came across a large volume called *The Record of the Irish International Exhibition of 1907*. Riffling through its pages, I realised how important this event was for Ireland, and for Dublin in particular.

I kept a keen interest in the exhibition and as time went on I accumulated sufficient material to be able to mount little exhibitions of my own on the Great White Fair. Then, about fifteen years ago, I was asked to give a slide show at the senior citizens' club, in the Red Cross centre on Newbridge Avenue, Sandymount, now called the Iris Charles Centre. I gathered together postcards of the 1907 exhibition and showed a few dozen slides. Halfway through the talk I put up a photograph of one of the most popular attractions at the exhibition, and jokingly commented that 'of course, no one here would remember going down the water chute'.

'Oh, I do,' came a voice from out of the darkness, 'and I was fifteen at the time.' There was silence for a few seconds before another voice said 'My god, she's a hundred!' From that moment my interest was aroused. The lady, who indeed was a centenarian, was Mrs Mary Murray of Sandymount, and she had a clear recollection of the exhibition. She granted me a few interviews and allowed me to take her photograph.

From then on I was completely fascinated by this exhibition and continued to add to my collection of postcards and memorabilia of the event. I discovered two plaster wall plaques belonging to my late father-in-law, Jack Geoghegan. My eldest son Gerard has helped with his forays on the internet and one precious souvenir of the exhibition was found in Christchurch, New Zealand. Indeed it was Gerard who chivvied me into searching through 'The Boxes', as my family call my chaotic collections, and it is for his expertise and encouragement in putting together this centenary book that I will be forever grateful.

Several other people helped me, knowingly and unknowingly, in this project. I have been a member of the Old Dublin Society for more than forty years and many of my fellow members have been generous with their time and expertise. The late Fred Dixon was a great authority on the event and the postcards published in conjunction with it. I thank Fred and his late wife Beatrice for all their help and generosity. My great friend Tony Behan also made his own collection available and some of his postcards appear within these pages. I also thank the late Martin Walton and Danny Parkinson, both of whom allowed me access to their collections over the years.

I acknowledge a debt to those that wrote about the exhibition, especially those anonymous reporters 'of the day', as well as the likes of Bram Stoker, Alfred Temple, Richard Tresilian, William Dennehy, and those who compiled the various publications that emerged from the exhibition itself. Fred Dixon and John Turpin have written about the event in the *Dublin Historical Record*, the journal of the Old Dublin Society, and I am grateful for their work which I quote from. Joseph Robins' book *Champagne and Buckles* was useful on the social scene that surrounded the vice-regal court. A short history of the exhibition I wrote appears in *The Roads to Sandymount, Irishtown and Ringsend* (1996) compiled by Sandymount Community Services, and I have drawn on that in this volume. I would also like to thank John Callanan, librarian of the Institute of Engineers, Clyde Road, for his information on Richard Tresilian, and the ever-helpful staff of the Gilbert Library, Pearse Street.

Thank you also to Peter Dunne, a distinguished old Dubliner whose proofreading skill has made this a better book than it might have been. Any mistakes that have slipped through are entirely my fault and I apologise for them.

I would like to dedicate this book to my wife Maureen who has, with great resignation, accepted the eccentricities of my lifestyle and pursuits for the last forty-six years.

Brian Siggins,
May 2007

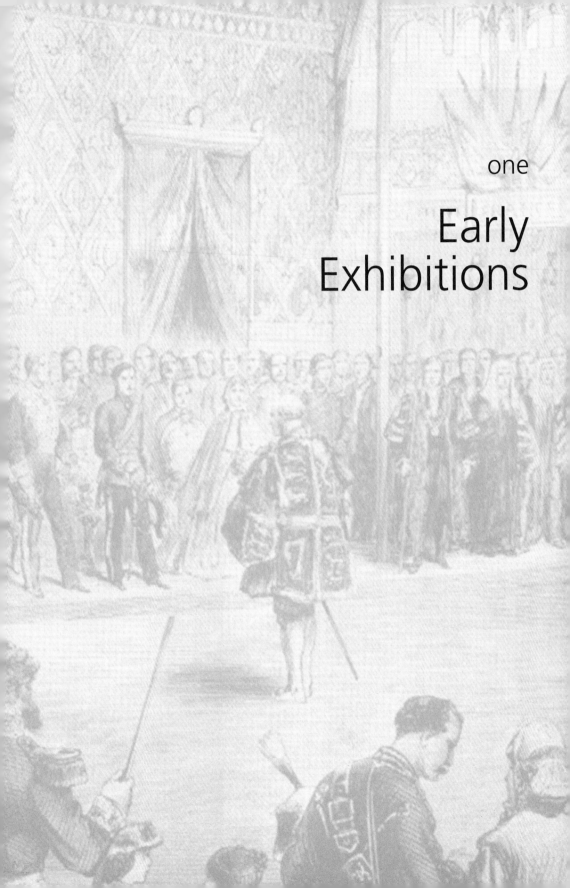

one

Early
Exhibitions

I OO^years ago, the landscape of the prosperous south Dublin villages of Ballsbridge and Donnybrook changed forever. On an unimpressive piece of scrubland between the two Pembroke Township hamlets a small city sprang up, grandiose buildings rose to the sky and a wonderful array of exhibits and attractions went on display. Almost three million people came to see what it was all about, many travelling from beyond the limits of the city and the shores of Ireland.

It was an extraordinary feat of organisation, and of entrepreneurship. It came about because of the vision of one man, the commitment of another and the management skills of a third. While the names of William Dennehy, William Martin Murphy and James Shanks are to the fore, there are many more known and unknown who contributed to making the Irish International Exhibition the sensation of 1907.

Their prime motivation was to reflect the thrusting spirit of the age and to highlight Irish industrial endeavour. The Irish entrepreneurial classes were itching to show the world what they could do, and also to discover what was going on in the world outside.

They brought in many hundreds of thousands of pounds to the city, boosting several sectors and increasing Ireland's profile internationally. Today, there are still relics of that summer that exist in Dublin 4. The exhibition buildings were made of wood, steel and plaster—and were removed shortly afterwards—but the lengthy pond that held the Canadian Water Chute was a memorable feature of the event. This water feature still forms a central position in Herbert Park, which itself was laid out after the exhibition closed and was presented to the public by the Earl of Pembroke.

International exhibitions were enormously important cultural and economic events that showcased the latest technologies and products in the era long before cinema, radio, television and electronic media. The first international exhibition was held in 1798, when the Commissioners of the Royal Manufactory of Les Gobelins and Sevres showed off their ceramics and silverware in Paris. The most celebrated was reputedly the idea of Prince Albert, husband of Queen Victoria and held in London, in 1851 under the title 'Great Exhibition of the Works of Industry of All Nations'. This is claimed to be the first in the United Kingdom, but the Royal Dublin Society beat them to it by two years.

As the idea developed, many other sections of industry and society became involved and art, tourism and education were showcased. The World's Fair concept spread and shows were held in Paris, Vienna, Philadelphia, Melbourne and many other cities. The 1904 World's Fair in St Louis inspired a celebrated Hollywood movie and title song, *Meet me in St Louis*, as well as enticing the nascent Olympic movement to hold its games there. Ireland was strongly represented at St Louis, with several schools renting stalls, including the Sandymount Academical Institution. Another school represented was my own lifelong place of employment, Pembroke, later Ringsend, Technical Institute which displayed inlaid cabinet and wrought-iron working. International exhibitions declined in importance after the Second World War but were reinvented as the more culturally-oriented Expo, now held every two or three years.

The Royal Dublin Society, founded in 1731, had used a system of awards to try to raise the standards in arts, crafts, farming and manufacturing, beginning with its first manufacturing exhibition in 1734. These were held on a one-acre site in Kildare Street every three years before

The Prince of Wales, a boy of eleven, opens the first Irish exhibition in 1853. More than half a century later he returned to Dublin for the Irish International Exhibition.

With his mother Queen Victoria still in mourning for her husband Albert, the Prince of Wales (later King Edward VII) opens Dargan's Irish Exhibition in Earlsfort Terrace, 1865.

THE

ILLUSTRATED RECORD

AND

DESCRIPTIVE CATALOGUE

OF THE

Dublin International Exhibition

OF

1865.

COMPILED AND EDITED BY

HENRY PARKINSON, BARRISTER-AT-LAW,
SECRETARY AND COMPTROLLER;
AND

PETER LUND SIMMONDS, F.S.S.,
COLONIAL SUPERINTENDENT;
AIDED BY

NUMEROUS CONTRIBUTIONS FROM THE SEVERAL HEADS OF DEPARTMENTS
AND OTHER EXPERIENCED WRITERS ON SPECIAL SUBJECTS.

With Two Hundred and Fifty Illustrations on Wood, Stone, and Steel; Photographs, &c.

PUBLISHED UNDER THE
EXECUTIVE

SANCTION OF THE
COMMITTEE.

LONDON:
E. AND F. N. SPON, 16, BUCKLERSBURY.
DUBLIN: JOHN FALCONER, 53, UPPER SACKVILLE-STREET.

1866.

Above: The fabled 'Crystal Palace' in London, home of the Great Exhibition of 1851.

Left: Frontispiece of the catalogue for the 1865 Dublin exhibition.

Opposite: The structure on Leinster lawn that housed the 1865 exhibition.

the first foreign exhibitors were invited in 1850. The RDS exhibitions lasted six months and were attended by about 300,000 people. Perhaps it was the success of the Dublin events that inspired Prince Albert, as the royals had visited Dublin in 1849.

The Hyde Park fair is best remembered for the striking signature building in which it was held, the Crystal Palace. The building, whose nickname was given to it by *Punch* magazine, was designed by Thomas Paxton, after he won a competition in which he beat the challenge of a Dubliner, Richard Turner. Turner owned an ironworks on Pembroke Road and he was commemorated by Turner's Cottages, a street demolished in the 1960s close to the UCD veterinary college. The fair concept spread rapidly, with Ireland's city of Cork hosting a six-month event in 1852, and the following year a million people attended the international exhibition that was held on the six-and-a-half acres of Leinster Lawn in Merrion Street.

This event was the idea of the engineer William Dargan who ended up bearing the losses of £19,000. Dargan had made his name, and his fortune, as a railway builder, laying more than 800 miles of track in Ireland, including the first route from Dublin to Kingstown (now Dun Laoghaire). A competition was held to design the building for the exhibition and was won by John Benson of Cork, whose entry was clearly influenced by Paxton's Crystal Palace. Benson's edifice was enormous; its largest section (425 feet by 100 feet and 100 feet high) was larger than Paxton's largest. Benson used wood instead of iron and eventually 2,530 tons of wood were used in the building, as well as 8 tons of putty and 70,000 square feet of glass. Some of the materials were salvaged afterwards and still survive in one of the glasshouses in the Botanic Gardens.

The 1853 exhibition was seen by 956,295 people and took in £29,000. It was similar to London in the range of its sections such as with Raw Materials, Machinery, Manufactures, and Fine Arts, but did not award medals or prizes to the entrants. A weekly newspaper was produced throughout the event and the twenty-five issues were compiled into a bound volume the following year.

Above and below: The water chute was a money spinner for the exhibition at Cork in 1903.

Queen Victoria and Prince Albert visited in August, and also visited Dargan at home in Mount Anville in Goatstown to offer him a baronetcy for his services. Dargan declined the offer but there was wide public feeling that he deserved some permanent tribute from his fellow citizens. A testimonial fund was established and the £5,000 raised was put towards a Public Gallery of Art which was opened in 1864 with a fine statue of Dargan overlooking the lawn.

Several small art exhibitions were held in Leinster Gardens over the next decade but building on the RDS site, including the art gallery, reduced the area available for exhibits and it was felt a new site would be needed for any further ambitious events.

The Dublin Exhibition Palace and Winter Garden Co. Ltd was floated as a joint stock undertaking in 1862 with a capital of £50,000. Its chairman was the Duke of Leinster and featured many prominent businessmen including Benjamin Guinness and John Switzer. They settled on a site on Earlsfort Terrace between St Stephen's Green and Hatch Street, known as the Coburg Gardens. These gardens had been popular in Georgian times, holding musical displays and firework shows, and had hosted cricket internationals in the 1850s, but had fallen into dereliction and by 1862 were being grazed on by sheep.

A competition was held to design a suitable building for the site, but many of the entries were not deemed worthy. The winning entrant, A.G. Jones, was asked to join forces with the company's own architect, Mr Darley, and create another design. Work commenced on the result of their labours in May 1863 and took two years to complete. The 17,100 square foot building now serves as the National Concert Hall.

The first exhibition was held in 1865, with medals awarded in the main categories of Raw Materials, Machinery, Textiles, Fine Arts and Metallic Vitreous and Ceramic Manufactures. Package tours were organised for visitors, with cheap excursion fares negotiated with railway companies all over Britain and even on the Continent. The local rail firms were less generous, but some cut-price fares were arranged. The Great South Western Railway brought over 10,000 passengers to Dublin, many for their first visit to the city, with fares such as the 2s 6d return from Carlow.

With Queen Victoria still mourning the death of Albert in 1861, the grand opening on 9 May was conducted by the Prince of Wales. This was the most cosmopolitan event yet held, with twenty-seven nations represented, with many entries from Zollverein, an economic union of many of the German states. The infamous name of Krupps appears on the list of medallists in one of the armament classes. A Mr Hercules McDonnell was sent around Europe to drum up interest in the exhibition and was shocked by the 'continentals'' view of Ireland as a land of terrorism, rebellion and oppression! An audience with the Pope led to several Roman sculptors sending works, although they were not popular with the Dublin public and sales were low. The overall attendance at the exhibition was 930,000 and profits were £10,000.

The event was also notable as the last public appearance of Sir William Rowan Hamilton, mathematician and astronomer. Hamilton was born in Dublin in 1805 and knighted in 1835, on the occasion of the first meeting in Dublin of the British Association. His works on the General System of Dynamics, Calculus of Quaternions, and his various contributions to philosophical transactions, are all testimony to his genius. He died on 2 September 1865, aged sixty.

Another exhibition was held at Earlsfort Terrace in 1872, but only 420,000 attended and the event had to be subvented by Lord Ardilaun and Lord Iveagh. The exhibition palace was considered a white elephant, with the Dublin wit Edwin Hamilton penning an ode to it in his *Dublin Doggerels* (1877):

> The Exhibition Palace was
> Comparatively little known
> When George the First was on the throne;
> And this is possibly because
> It wasn't built until after then.
> From this we learn that early kings
> Dispensed with multitudes of things
> That even ordinary men
> In latter times may call their own –
> Or rather visit now and then

Because the Palace is again
Comparatively little known
Its name, however, still remains
On tramway-cars which never go
To it, but stop at Westland Row
For the arrival of the trains.

In 1882 the buildings were purchased by the government and the grounds returned to the Guinness family, at which point they were renamed the Iveagh Gardens. The government decided that the palace was the ideal home for the new Royal University which had replaced the Dublin Castle-based Queen's University in 1880. In 1914 it was taken over by the National University but after UCD moved to Belfield in the 1960s and 1970s it was turned into a National Concert Hall, which opened in 1981. The three statues that stood over the entrance hall of the 1865 exhibition stood until early 2007 in the small garden beside City Hall in Dame Street.

A new company, the Irish Exhibition Co. Ltd, was founded in 1882 by a group that included the Lord Mayor of Dublin. While the 1862 company had been formed by a small group of big businessmen, the 1882 entity was much more widely-based, with hundreds of small shareholders. They were not granted use of Earlsfort Terrace, but quickly found an alternative site at the Rotunda Gardens, in what is now Parnell Square. The exhibition was opened on 15 August, the same day that the Daniel O'Connell statue was unveiled at the other end of Sackville Street. It was very late in the year to start such a venture and, although it remained open until early January, it failed to draw the crowds. The north inner city was less fashionable than the thriving southern suburbs and just 261,000 paid admissions were recorded.

Several smaller exhibitions were held in Earlsfort Terrace, such as that organised by the Arts and Crafts Society in 1899. The celebrated Trinity wit, John Pentland Mahaffy (who had played cricket for Ireland on the site in 1861), wrote the speech for the Lord Lieutenant:

Right: William Martin Murphy, the controversial businessman who was chairman of the powerful Finance Committee.

Opposite: The Irish schools' display at the World's Fair in St Louis in 1904. Several Dublin educational establishments, including Pembroke Technical School, exhibited at the fair.

In the cultivation of beauty, not only in its loftier sense, but on the practical side, by proper designs, by proper adapting of means to ends, by combining simplicity with elegance, every man and woman, nay, even every intelligent youth, can help to make our life better and purer, and therefore happier; for here the many and the few, the poor and the rich, the native and the settler, the producer and the employer, can combine and contribute to their country's good.

Another enormous event was staged in the Royal Dublin Society show grounds in Ballsbridge in May 1902. Given the title of *Gigas* (Greek for 'giant'), it was a series of fundraising activities for the City of Dublin Hospital in Baggot Street. The giant bazaar included stalls representing the countries of the world and dozens of extraordinary entertainments: trick cycling, conjurors, a haunted room, golf driving, Mrs Hawtrey Benson's Temple of Repose, the White Coons, riding in a motor car and demonstrations of x-rays. While the RDS grounds still host an annual funfair, one cannot imagine many of the above finding favour at twenty-first-century Funderland.

Ireland was strongly represented at the World's Fair in St Louis, with full-scale models of St Lawrence's Gate in Drogheda, Cormac's Chapel from the Rock of Cashel, the keep of Blarney Castle and the big cross at Monasterboice. The restaurant in the Irish section was a model, with windows, of the Bank of Ireland on College Green. An enormous number of Irish products – filling 805 packing cases – were shipped over under the auspices of Sir Horace Plunkett and the Department of Agriculture and Technical Instruction.

In 1901 the then Lord Mayor of Cork, Edward Fitzgerald, proposed that an International Industrial Exhibition be staged in the city in the following year. The city had hosted a successful Industrial and Fine Arts Exhibition in 1883 and Fitzgerald's idea was greeted enthusiastically and a site was chosen on an area of parkland between the Cork County cricket grounds on the Mardyke and what is now Thomas Davis Bridge.

Among the attractions were an enormous water chute and a switchback railway, while the grounds were laid out with pavilions, kiosks, tea houses and ornamental walks. Cork organised

a creditable exhibition, but was limited by the capital available, a sum less than £30,000. Its industrial, artistic and agricultural sections attracted exhibitors from all over the world. It ran from 1 May to 1 November and exceeded all expectations. It was then decided to do it all again the following year, when it was visited by Edward VII and Queen Alexandra, and that most eminent Victorian, cricketer W.G. Grace.

The Cork International Exhibition finally closed on 31 October 1903 and its instigator, Edward Fitzgerald, was made a Baronet by Edward VII. The grounds were donated to Cork Corporation as a recreational park for the citizens, and were named Fitzgerald's Park.

Those recent, highly successful World's Fairs in Chicago (1893) and Paris (1900), and the Cork exhibition, acted as an inspiration to William T. Dennehy, who proposed setting up an International Exhibition in Dublin.

Dennehy was editor of the *Irish Independent* when, in January 1903, he wrote a series of articles expressing the need for co-ordination of the current widespread efforts ('The Industrial Awakening') to spread co-operation in agriculture and industry. He advocated a National Institute for Commerce and Industries and pressed for preparations to be made for another International Exhibition to be held in Dublin. Dennehy's articles made waves and several important gentlemen sent letters of support to his newspaper. A 'semi-public' meeting was held in the Shelbourne Hotel on 4 February 1903, with invitations sent out by Dennehy and Lord Castletown, 'to consider the advisability of taking steps to hold, at an early stage, an Industrial Conference, constituted on non-sectarian and non-political lines'.

The proposal had the backing of the Lord Lieutenant, the Earl of Dudley, and on the eve of the meeting his Chief Secretary, George Wyndham MP, had a letter published:

I felt last summer, and said, at the Cork Exhibition, that there was a new breath of hope and energy stirring the atmosphere of Irish enterprise. That impression has since been deepened

The Water Chute
Scottish National Exhibition, Edinburgh, 1908.

Opposite and above: Water chutes were popular attractions at exhibitions, such as these in New Zealand (1906) and Edinburgh (1908).

Right: The Marquess of Ormonde, Vice-Admiral James Edward William Theobald Butler, who was president of the exhibition.

and confirmed. No one will rejoice more sincerely than I if the meeting on tomorrow leads many to see that, with the advent, of new conditions affecting the problems of production and transport, there is the chance of Ireland finding herself less severely handicapped than heretofore in the peaceable rivalry of commerce. It will, at any rate, be admitted that it is the duty of all who would assist Ireland to discover whether the chance exists and if – as I believe – it does, to seize it.

The Irish Industrial Conference was held on 15 April 1903 in the Royal University, Earlsfort Terrace, chaired by W.J. Pirrie of Harland and Wolff Shipbuilders, Belfast. Hundreds of interested parties attended, and all were listed in the subsequent record of the exhibition. There were ten peers, seventeen MPs (including the Lord Mayor of Dublin, Tim Harrington, a leading member of the Home Rule party at Westminster), a dozen baronets (including the Dublin-born captain of the English cricket team, Sir Timothy Carew O'Brien), eighteen knights, dozens of Lord Lieutenants, a handful of bishops of all persuasions, and hundreds of representatives of local authorities throughout the land. The Lord Mayor of Cork exhorted the attendance to 'take off their coats and get to work', asking them why it was that no Irish manufacturer could make a boot to fit Irish feet.

Lord Castletown acknowledged that Ireland was not moving as fast as other countries, but pointed to Pirrie as a 'great captain of industry' and suggested that the work of Horace Plunkett, who sent his apologies, be supplemented. Irishmen went to America to work, and worked hard there; 'why not work at home?' he asked.

Many more speeches were made but only one important resolution was adopted, unanimously, that there should be a Dublin International Exhibition. Those who spoke in favour of this included the Lord Mayors of Dublin and Cork as well as the President of the Dublin Trades Council, the High Sheriff and the Chairman of the Dublin County Council. The resolution stated that the government should be requested to provide a suitable site in the Phoenix Park.

A company with the title 'Irish International Exhibition (Incorporated)' was set up under the Limited Liabilities Act. A committee was formed – it held its first meetings in the Mansion House just a week after the Earlsfort Terrace conference – and began the process of examining potential sites.

The government was approached for a site in the Phoenix Park, and the subcommittee examined the various sites. Three possible sites were identified, one running north from Parkgate Street to the Phoenix Column, from the Zoological Gardens to the gates of the Viceregal Lodge and including the polo grounds; a second ran south from the cricket clubs to the Magazine Fort; the third was also on the south side of the park, overlooking the boat clubs on the Liffey. However the transport infrastructure was poor in the region of the park and it was later abandoned for a south side venue.

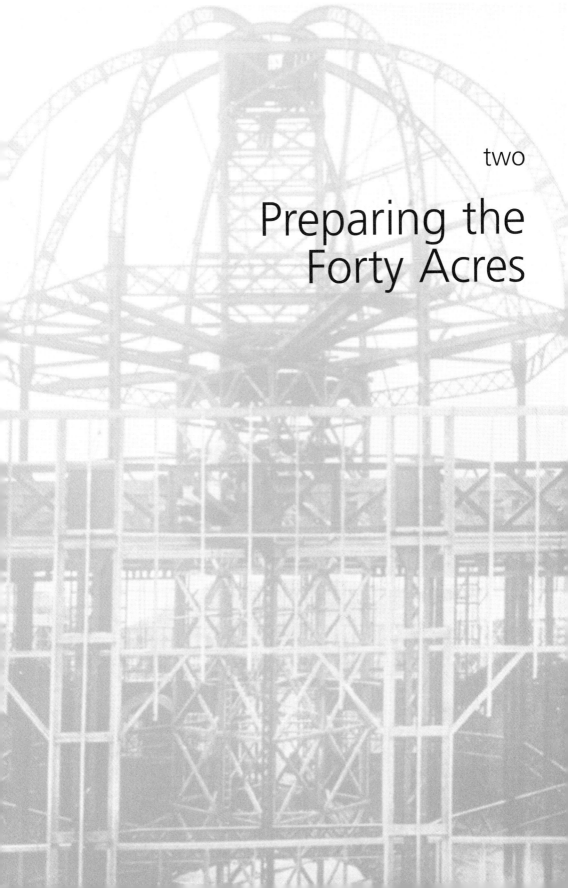

two

Preparing the
Forty Acres

The committee next identified an area of rough ground in Ballsbridge lying between the River Dodder, Morehampton Road and Clyde Road, as a possible venue. The site's proximity to the main tram line from the city centre, and the Dublin-Wicklow-Waterford rail line would have been a key attraction, especially as some key officials of the transport companies were to the fore among the exhibition organisers.

The site was known as the Forty Acres, a name it had borne since the thirteenth century, and had been promised by the Earl of Pembroke to the Pembroke District Council as a public park to mark his son Herbert reaching the age of twenty-one. Some committee members met Mr Fane Vernon of the Pembroke Estate who told them that if the PDC could be induced to waive their claim on the land for the duration of the exhibition, the Earl of Pembroke would look favourably on their request.

Francis Erlington Ball wrote, in a guidebook produced to mark the Exhibition:

A year ago the site was pasture land, the one oasis left in the western portion of the Pembroke Township. Although preparations were being made for its conversion into a public park, the ground still presented a most rural appearance, even preserving some remnants of the primitive fences, consisting of mud banks surmounted by thorn hedges, which formerly bordered the road from Dublin to Donnybrook. So long as it remained, this green spot served to remind the passer-by that the suburb in which the International Exhibition has been erected is a modern extension of Dublin, and that Donnybrook and Ball's Bridge were of old time far removed from city life.

On 28 July the subcommittee met a delegation from the Pembroke Council. The council's chairman, Sir Robert Gardner, stated frankly that they would only accede to the request when they were assured that the exhibition company's financial resources were adequate. He also pointed out that the council would be forced to construct two roads to facilitate the event, at a total cost of £3,500, which he believed should be the sum the exhibition would pay as tenants. When the council members left, the subcommittee decided to immediately prepare an outline scheme for an exhibition at Herbert Park.

A plan was drawn up by George Ashlin and John H. Ryan which also included a sports stadium on the site of the present Leinster Branch rugby grounds in Donnybrook. Their plan was not adopted, although Dennehy acknowledged that its publication in the press played a huge part in convincing the public that the exhibition was a serious idea.

A contemporary report ran as follows:

No more suitable position could have been chosen than the park of fifty-two acres, and special interest attaches to the site by reason of the fact that it includes a large tract of naturally wooded land lately presented to the Pembroke Urban District by the Right Hon. The Earl of Pembroke, in commemoration of the coming of age of his son, Lord Herbert. At the close of the Exhibition, this part of the ground will be thrown open to the public as a park and recreation ground forever.

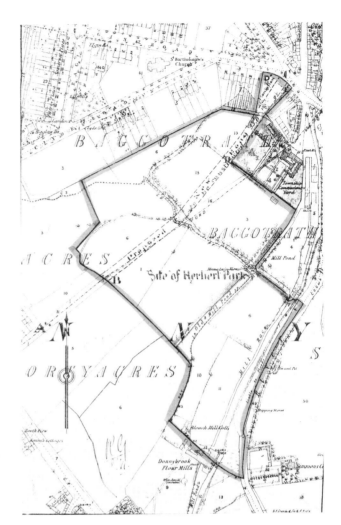

Right: Map of the Ballsbridge/
Donnybrook area, with the area
occupied by Herbert Park outlined
in bold.

Below: The pavilions begin to take
shape.

There was a natural pond on the wasteland of the Forty Acres, but this shows the construction of the pond that survives to this day.

The Pavilion of Fine Arts begins to take shape.

The steel frame work of the Grand Central Palace was surrounded with wood and plaster.

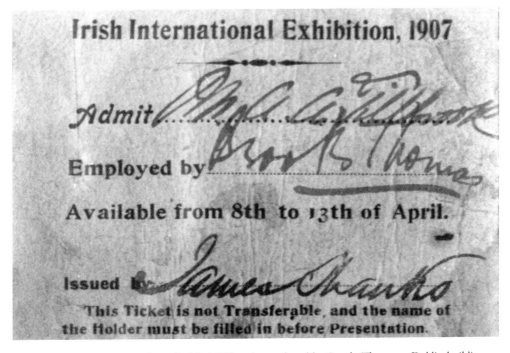

This pass was issued to a worker called A.A. Tilbrook, employed by Brooks Thomas, a Dublin building supplier that still operates today.

A further thirteen acres between Morehampton Road and Herbert Park, owned by Mrs Sullivan and Colonel Heppesley, were secured for the term of three years at £400 per annum.

The next move was to raise the vast sum that would be required, and donations and loans were sought. A public meeting was held on 22 February 1904 at which an appeal was made. There was an unsavoury incident at this meeting when voices were raised by a breakaway faction who wanted to organise a *national* exhibition. Some of the original movers in the international exhibition meetings had decided that a local focus was required and set up their own organisation, which eventually collapsed.

As preparations continued to be made, it became clear to the organising committee that they were on their own. It had been expected that a Royal Commission would be appointed to take over the administration of the event. However, as the official record put it, 'the committee had been unduly sanguine in relying on receiving liberal and practical assistance from the Treasury'.

The problem for the committee now was that they would have to work a lot harder than they expected, and with far greater responsibility hanging over their heads. The record complained that 'it was daily becoming more apparent that the heads of the Irish government were evincing disinclination to give monetary aid on a scale worthy of the undertaking to which the Committee was pledged'.

In April 1904 it was decided to throw open the Guarantee Fund to all and sundry. An address was written and circulated widely. The document described the exhibition's scope, the financial support needed and the steps already taken to secure it. It also promised that:

> All the work at the Exhibition will, as far as possible, be executed of Irish material by Irish workmen, and as the primary object of those who are engaged in this enterprise is the

W. Kaye-Parry, the consulting architect to the exhibition.

James Shanks, the dynamic Chief Executive
Officer who drove the ambitious project.

Joseph Mooney QC, a leading member of the
Executive Council.

advancement of Irish industry, a special Committee will be formed whose duty will be, among others, to reserve the most prominent position in the Exhibition for the display of Irish Manufactures ... In order to accomplish the truly patriotic objects they have set before them, the Committee now confidently appeal to all Irishmen and friends of Ireland to join in the guarantee, and so enable them to raise the necessary funds for carrying out their great enterprise.

A committee meeting on the 26th of that month reported that the guarantee fund stood at £69,870, but a subcommittee formed to look into the advisability of hiring a project manager reported back their approval of the idea. They recommended hiring James Shanks, JP, for an initial period of six months.

The president of the International Exhibition was the Most Honourable the Marquess of Ormonde, KP, State Steward to the Lord Lieutenant, while the various publications listed forty-two vice-presidents and fifty-three members of the Executive Council, which was presided over by Lord Castletown. These gentlemen, and they were all men, included dozens of Earls, Lords and Knights, as well as the leading industrialists of the day. Many of the names

The skeleton of the giant dome begins to take shape.

Opposite: Inside the dome of the Grand Central Palace, as construction nears completion.

still survive in the city attached to their respective businesses: Cochrane, Goulding, Jameson, Battersby, Bewley, Conyngham, Findlater and Jury.

Chairman of the powerful Finance and General Purposes Committee was William Martin Murphy, who had bought the *Irish Independent* in 1903. Murphy owned many businesses but it was his ownership of the tramway system in Dublin which was to add to his fortune as the crowds flocked to the suburb to visit the exhibition. The *Irish Independent* and the recently-founded *Sunday Independent* eagerly reported on the progress of the exhibition. Murphy, an MP from 1885-92, is an enormously controversial figure in Irish history, chiefly due to his leadership of the Dublin employers in a dispute with the Jim Larkin-led trade unions which led to a lockout in 1913.

Ormonde, Murphy and their many subcommittees soon had an army of 1,500 men preparing the 52 acres, which stretched from Ballsbridge to Morehampton Road, and from the bank of the Dodder River to Clyde Road. Much of the area was rough ground, although some ancient trees helped give the site some grandeur.

On 5 May 1906, *The Irish Times* reported on the 'Progress of the Buildings', stating that barely six weeks had passed since the first sod was cut for the main halls but that by then a skeleton framework was in place on three of them and the foundations laid for the fourth.

The excitement felt among the citizens of Dublin was not unanimous. *Conradh na Gaeilge*, the Gaelic League, opposed the exhibition and called it 'The Police Aided Exhibition'. Their objection was on the grounds that the exhibition would bring in foreign goods and do little to increase home manufactures. *Conradh* proposed that a national exhibition be held which would showcase indigenous industry and exhibit some former trades which had died out. It also suggested that Ireland's underdeveloped resources be highlighted, with overseas examples of how they might be developed. It also proposed sections on Irish arts, handicrafts, agriculture, horticulture, forestry, peat, mining and fisheries. As it turned out, many of these sectors would feature in the exhibition.

Shanks threw himself into the role with gusto, although his initial progress was slow and he pulled in just £3,600 in the first eight months.

By 19 July 1904 the fund was up to £92,828, and two months later stood at £103,270. However as the exhibition neared he was able to secure large guarantees from transport companies such as the Dublin United Tramway Company (£12,500) and the Great Northern Railway and Great Southern and Western Railway (£5,000 each), all of whom clearly stood to reap much benefit from a successful exhibition. Other major benefactors were Lord Iveagh (£1,000 cash plus guarantee of £10,000) and Arthur Guinness, Son & Co. Ltd (£5,000 guarantee).

Shanks was also able to report to the committee in May 1905 that the contractors, Messrs Humphreys Ltd of Knightsbridge, London, had expressed willingness to sign a guarantee for £25,000 (later increased to £26,000) in the event of their plans and estimates for the construction of the Exhibition buildings being approved and the contract placed with them. This eccentric arrangement allowed the committee to raise the Guarantee Fund total to £131,865. Shanks also said he was confident of doing similar deals with other contractors.

The satisfactory progress of the financial arrangements was reflected in this letter to Robert Gardner from William Martin Murphy and W.F. Bolton:

23rd June 1905   39 Dame Street, Dublin

Dear Mr Gardner,
Referring to our interview with you yesterday, we are able to assure you that the Exhibition Project is now within measurable distance of success.
The possession of the site is essential to enable the Committee to mature their plans, and as to

the suggestion that they might retain the lands for an undue period without proceeding with the undertaking, we desire to say that nothing can be further from the wish or intention of anybody connected with the Exhibition Project. To meet such an objection we undertake that in the event of the Pembroke Council not being satisfied before the 1st January 1906 that the guarantees for £150,000 have been obtained, and that the Bankers were willing to make the necessary advances thereon, the ground shall be surrendered to the Pembroke Council and the deposit forfeited.

We are satisfied that the comparatively small sum now required to complete the guarantees for £150,000. would be readily forthcoming if the Committee were able to announce that they had obtained possession of the site, as the public interest in the Exhibition Project would be greatly stimulated thereby.

Yours faithfully,
W M Murphy
W F Bolton
(Attached an indenture made on 27th June 1905)

By September 1905 Shanks had the fund up to £150,178, and a week later added a £1,000 to that figure. However, there was some delay chasing up signatures and it wasn't until 10 January 1906 that he was able to hand over validly-executed guarantees totalling £150,702. The magic number of £150,000 had been passed, enabling the committee to sign the deal with the Pembroke estate. The final guarantee total was £153,375 5s, while guarantees for another £3,250 were retained by the committee. We can't be sure whether the thousand who invested in the exhibition were optimistic about possible profits, but in the end they received about one-third of their money back.

The original plan was to hold the event in 1906, but once work got underway it was put back to 1907. An English firm, Humphrey's of London and Dublin, was given the contract to develop the grounds, which naturally caused consternation. The firm had extensive experience of working on such events, notably at Paris and South Kensington, and was directed locally by George Freeman. The consulting architects were a local firm, Kaye-Parry Ross, who also designed Blackrock Baths, the Iveagh Buildings, Pembroke Library and Archer's Garage.

The exhibition buildings were made of iron girder frames covered with wood and plaster, and painted white. Although the corrugated iron was imported from England because it was not manufactured in Ireland, all the timber was sourced locally and all those who worked on the building were Irish. During construction one man, Francis Mooney, was killed.

The erection of the buildings was quite a challenge, with the enormous Grand Central Palace reaching 200 feet in diameter internally, its pivot-octagonal hall surmounted by a steel dome. From the main hall stretched out four radial halls, each 160 feet long by 80 feet wide. This building was constructed from 48,000 cubic feet of timber, 14,000 feet of sash-bars, 300 tons of steel, 70 tons of galvanised iron sheets and 22,000 feet of plate glass.

The second most important building was the Gallery of Fine Arts, which was divided into seven compartments. The Palace of Industries which rose up on the Northern side of the Central Palace, close to Morehampton Road, was 300 yards long and 100 feet wide. Next to the Palace of Industries ran the highway through the park, which after the visit of King Edward became known as Royal Avenue, and is now known simply as 'Herbert Park'. On the other side of this road lay the Canadian Pavilion.

The main entrance hall was at the junction of Pembroke and Clyde Road. Behind the façade lay the turnstiles and a colonnade of about eighty feet square in which stood the ticket offices and lost property office. From this led a gently-rising covered way, stretching sixty yards and thirteen yards wide, which led to a broad plateau from which three wide stairways and two slopes led to the great Celtic Court, which measured sixty-two yards by thirty yards. On either side of the main entrance hall, at the end nearest to the Grand Central Palace, stood the Concert Hall and the Popular Restaurant. The concert hall was a spacious building, measuring 170 feet by 80 feet and containing a large orchestra and organ loft.

The Popular Restaurant was managed by Lyons & Co. Ltd, as was its *de luxe* counterpart, the Palace Restaurant. This contained a series of four dining halls. Also in this building were the apartments provided for the King and Queen for their visit to the exhibition. According to the record:

> It was furnished and decorated in the highest taste, and was the fashionable rendezvous of the inhabitants of and visitors to Dublin throughout the existence of the Exhibition. Verandahs and balconies afforded, in warm weather, charming opportunities for lunching, dining or supping in the open air.

In the space between the Palace Restaurant and the Grand Central Palace lay a specially constructed pond above which the Canadian Water Chute soared. Next to the bandstand was the Home Industries Pavilion, which included two separate halls, and close by were the model village hall, the model village hospital and the model artisans' and labourers' cottages. The other buildings included the Open-air Tea Room, an Excursionist's Dining Room, ten bars or canteens, a number of lavatories and 'a handsome suite of Executive Offices', including a council room. Also erected was a great Power House which housed the enormous 'Dreadnought' tubular boilers which conducted the light and power around the buildings and grounds, and was overseen by the Resident Engineer, George Marshall Harris.

A public inspection of the site was hosted on 17 July 1906, with invitations issued to 'the more important guarantors', a large number of leading citizens, members of the various committees, the principal exhibitors and the representatives of 'all the more important journals of Great Britain, Ireland and the Continent'. More than 800 turned up to see what had been achieved to date. Lunch was served in the North Hall of the Central Palace after photographs were taken and an inspection of the buildings lasting just forty-five minutes was conducted.

The Marquess of Ormonde reported the King's best wishes to the exhibition, while James Shanks also made an official statement of the progress thus far achieved. Justice Ross rose to toast the Irish International Exhibition, stating that:

> Every Irishman had, deep down in his heart, an intense desire to do some good for Ireland. They all had one desire which they hoped to see gratified, and that was that Ireland should take her place amongst the other peoples of the earth as an industrial people.

William Martin Murphy replied to the toast with an explanation that he was speaking as Chairman of the Finance and General Purposes Committee, and that he was not in that position by any desire of his own, but because he was forced into it by 'circumstances to which I do not intend to allude'. These circumstances caused a difficulty which made the prospects of successfully carrying out the exhibition 'unpromising and hazardous'. However, 'being, I am afraid, of a rather pugnacious nature, I took up the stand I did in order to help the undertaking to success'.

Murphy assured the throng that the motives that prompted the exhibition were the purest: 'We had no object in view but the good of the country.' Murphy cited the example of Arthur Chamberlain, head of Kynoch & Co., who told how he had been warned about coming to establish an industry in Ireland:

He was told it would be ruinous, and that it could not succeed … the Irishman could not work, that he was not amenable to discipline, and that he had too many holidays, and that he could not get on with the priests.

Chamberlain went on to tell Murphy that, 'The Irishman worked quite as well as the Englishman, although he required, perhaps, a little more teaching, but he was a much pleasanter fellow to deal with than the Englishman.' And as for the priests, 'they gave me every assistance, invited me to every dinner, and my head still aches when I think of their hospitality'.

A Colonel Hutcheson-Poe said that some people had said that Ireland had nothing to gain and everything to lose as they were only inviting failure by drawing comparisons between their own commodities and those of their neighbours. The reverse is true he insisted – Ireland had nothing to fear.

More evidence of the rapid development of the site came in September 1906 when the annual conference of the Institute of Journalists was held in Dublin. The committee took advantage of the presence of a large number of writers and laid on a lunch. Several of the great and good were enlisted to court the reporters and a tour of the site was organised. William Martin Murphy gave a speech of welcome to the journalists 'and their lady friends', while Trinity provost Anthony Traill gave a witty speech. Joseph Mooney spoke too, and hinted at the problems the organisers had encountered. 'We encountered a great deal of opposition in the beginning from good, earnest Irishmen, who thought the project would be injurious to Ireland instead of doing good.' He admitted that they had received 'more kicks than ha'pence'. Murphy returned to pay tribute to the journalists, saying that he had mixed with journalists for the greater part of his lifetime, 'and a more amiable, more worthy and more loyal set of men he had never met in any walk of life'. The result of all this hospitality was vital publicity for the exhibition throughout Britain, its colonies, the continent and America. A special press room was installed in Ballsbridge and many journalists travelled to report on the exhibition. As one of the stated aims of the enterprise was to draw the world's attention to Dublin, it proved quite a success.

An eminent Irishman turned up in early 1907 to witness the finishing touches. Abraham 'Bram' Stoker was commissioned by the *World's Work* magazine to run his eye over the exhibition. Coining the phrase 'The Great White Fair', he waxed lyrical, 'Given a clear sky of Irish blue and a soft summer sun, one could well imagine oneself in the heart of Italy, or even in the still more luminous atmosphere of the Orient.' He predicted that the exhibition would help rehabilitate the name of the district: 'It is a far cry from this glittering vista to the latter days of the Donnybrook Fair, which forty years ago was accustomed to make this neighbourhood ill-famed throughout the world.'

Stoker hailed the passing of the era of the stage Irishman and of unrest between landlord and tenant, and asserted that 'there has come in its place a strenuous, industrious spirit, spreading its revivifying influence so rapidly over the old country as to be worth more than even historical bitterness'. The author of *Dracula* pointed out that Ireland was well-placed to reap a benefit from the attention:

The geographical position of the island, which stands as the outpost on the Western sea; its isolation, emphasised by the neglect of many centuries; and, from the nature of its natural products, a logical lack of transport facilities – all have tended to create for its inhabitants a personal ignorance both of itself and of the outside world.

Stoker visited the site, amazed at the improvements wrought:

> In the fifties … it was a more or less an uninviting waste on the ragged edge of an unimportant stream, best known as the site of Donnybrook Fair (whose) very name became a synonym for misconduct. I remember an expression which I often heard used of it in my own youth: 'The Devil would be in Hell only for Donnybrook'. At last it became such an evil that it had to be abolished.

Stoker paid tribute to James Shanks, Secretary to the Committee and the Exhibition's Chief Executive Officer, who he credited as the man 'who has done more than any one other man to carry the undertaking through'. The division of labour was that Murphy 'devoted himself unreservedly to the direction and supervision of the works and general organisation of the Exhibition', while Shanks 'devolved the labour and responsibility of carrying on the general business of the exhibition from hour to hour, and of dealing with the enormous amount of detail which could not possibly be allowed to lie over for the consideration of the committee.' The committee suffered a serious blow shortly after the exhibition opened with the death of the vice-chairman of the Finance and General Purposes Committee, Vere Ward Brown. His role was taken over by Alderman Irwin and later by Robert Booth.

Hundreds of thousands of promotional booklets were printed and distributed throughout Ireland, Britain and beyond, pointing out how technology had reduced distances:

> The Channel which divides Ireland from England has terrors no longer for the most timid traveller, and no holiday trip can be ventured upon more confidently, as the finest Channel Steamers in the world bridge the distance in two and three-quarter hours. Ireland, inhabited by a race noted for hospitality, receives with open hearts and hands all who visit her, and a *cead mile failthe* awaits all who visit her great Exhibition in 1907.

It was also pointed out that a journey from Euston to Westland Row, a total of 334½ miles, could be now completed in a little over nine hours.

By April 1907 most of the main structures were complete. The main entrance at Ballsbridge presented a gleaming white appearance with a large, arched doorway surmounted by two giant domes on either side. This structure towered eighty feet above the roadway and stretched across from where Roly's Bistro now stands to the American Embassy. An avenue led to the main feature, the Grand Central Palace, with its dome soaring 150 feet into the sky, covering 2.5 acres and leading out into four wings, each representing an Irish province. The other exhibition buildings, although not as large as the Central Palace, were still impressive, even by modern standards. The Palace of Mechanical Arts was 900 feet by 100 feet, while the Palace of Fine Arts occupied 33,000 square feet and the Palace of Industries 52,000 square feet. In all 1,100 tons of plaster were used and 250,000 yards of canvas. Dockrell's accounts revealed they had used 200 tons of rolled plate glass.

The respective cost of each of the buildings was accounted for separately:

Central Palace and Band Stand	£33,749
Main Entrance, Celtic Court, Concert Hall and Popular Restaurant	£15,208
Palace of the Mechanical Arts	£13,380
Palace of the Fine Arts	£7,948
Palace of Industries	£7,991

IRISH INTERNATIONAL EXHIBITION,
in course of Construction. To be Opened on May 4th. 1907.
by HIS EXCELLENCY THE LORD LIEUTENANT

A postcard advertises the imminent opening of the exhibition.

Palace Restaurant	£6,473
Catering offices, kitchens and bakeries	£4,785
Irish Home Industries Building	£2,356
Gas Pavilion	£2,523
Lake, Bridges and Temple on the island	£3,676
Water Chute	£3,241

The total amount spent on the buildings and enclosure of the exhibition was £118,061, to which was added another £5,600 for plumbing, lavatories, hire of turnstiles, architects and surveyors' fees and the salary of the Clerk of Works.

As the record of the exhibition stated:

> The committee had taken over possession of Herbert Park in what was practically a state of nature, and this of a very wild kind. The ground was wholly undrained; in winter or wet weather large tracts were little better than marshes or swamps.

A total of £3,660 was spent on drainage and £17,106 on roads and paths. The total spent on development and decoration of the grounds was £25,900. By the standards of the times this was an enormous amount of money. Murphy and his committee must have been nervous that their Great White Fair would turn out to be a great white elephant. With the enterprise ready for customers, it was time to open the doors.

three

The Grand Opening

On Wednesday 1 May, the Dublin daily newspapers printed an official notification from Sir Arthur E. Vicars, the Ulster King of Arms, which announced that there would be a state opening by the Lord Lieutenant, and listed in great detail the order of ceremonies of the day, the music that would be played and the order in which the various dignitaries would process from Dublin Castle to the exhibition grounds.

From an early hour on the 4 May crowds began assembling at both the Ballsbridge and Morehampton Road entrances to the exhibition. The organisation was perfect and stewards conducted the VIP guests to their allotted seats in the concert hall. Although the day was sunny, it was 'abnormally cold, with something like a small hurricane blowing'. It was to prove a harbinger of the summer as a whole.

Back in the city the Lord Lieutenant, Lord Aberdeen, and his wife Ishbel, were getting ready for the ceremonies. Before he left Dublin Castle he received a telegram from Paris saying, 'Trust that the Exhibition you are to open to-day may prove a success, and demonstrate International progress made by Ireland'. It was signed 'Edward R'. Just before he left he donned the insignia of the Grand Master of the Order of St Patrick, the fabled Irish Crown jewels. When he returned to the exhibition with his King later in the summer, those jewels would be absent, presumed stolen.

The Aberdeens rode in the third of three open carriages that set off at 11.15 a.m. along Dame Street, College Green, Grafton Street, St Stephen's Green and Leeson Street to the exhibition entrance on Morehampton Road in Donnybrook. On arrival at 11.45 a.m. they went straight to the Concert Hall for the official opening in front of 2,000 people.

The hall was decorated 'elaborately and lavishly'. Its doors had opened at 10 a.m. sharp and had been closed at 11.30 a.m. when it was filled 'to the rafters'. *The Irish Times* reported that:

> Rarely before has such a gathering been witnessed in the metropolis … Here were representatives of every interest and every class in Ireland. Officers in gorgeous uniforms mingled in pleasing contrast with those who were attired in sombre morning dress, while the picturesqueness of the scene was completed by the delightful costumes of the ladies, who had gathered in hundreds.

At noon the Exhibition Executive Council and Committee entered, again in strict order as ordained by Arthur Vicars, followed by a fanfare of trumpets to herald the arrival of the viceregal party. The band welcomed them with *God Save the King* and the march, 'Hail, Bright Abode' from *Tannhäuser*, followed by the overture to the same piece by Wagner. There were no fewer than 600 performers in the orchestra, band and chorus led by Patrick Delaney and under the musical direction of the famed Irish tenor Barton M'Guckin who had sung at Covent Garden and La Scala.

The Marquess of Ormonde read from an illuminated address, written on vellum, welcoming the Lord Lieutenant, who replied by reading from the telegram he had received that morning from the King. The official report related that 'the reading of the Royal message was loudly cheered, and it was several minutes before Lord Aberdeen could proceed'. Lord Aberdeen pointed out that the sovereign's interest was not only:

IRISH INTERNATIONAL EXHIBITION.

President:
The Most Hon. The Marquess of Ormonde, K.P.

The President & Council request the honour of the presence of

Mr Frengley & Lady

in the Concert Hall of the Exhibition on Saturday 4th May 1907.
on the occasion of the State Opening of the Exhibition by
His Excellency the Earl of Aberdeen, K.T. Lord Lieutenant of Ireland,
and The Countess of Aberdeen.

Herbert Park.
Dublin.

James Shanks,
Chief Executive Officer.

A prized invitation to the opening, issued to a Mr Frengley 'and Lady'. This individual may have been Jacob, a jeweller from Crow Street, or Joseph of 64 Ranelagh Road.

The viceregal party arrive by horse-drawn carriage.

The enormous 800-strong choir and orchestra perform at the opening ceremony.

The Marquess of Ormonde reads a welcoming address to Lord Aberdeen.

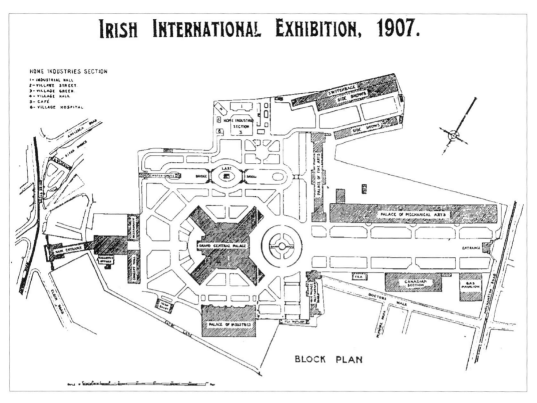

Map showing the exhibits at an early stage. Some of the pavilions, such as the French, do not appear on this map. The exhibition eventually occupied fifty-two acres.

… gratifying, but decidedly significant. King Edward is ever ready to identify himself with the interests and concerns of the people over whom he presides, and the people of Ireland have not been slow to recognise and appreciate the warm, sympathetic interest evinced by the King regarding this country – and in this spontaneous greeting we have a further indication of that solicitude.

Gordon John Campbell, the seventh Earl of Aberdeen, was in his second term in the Viceregal Lodge, following a brief spell in 1886. His second sojourn lasted from 1905-1915, the longest term served by a viceroy. Aberdeen was a convinced Home Ruler, and had annoyed many loyalists when he discarded much of the ceremonial and flummery associated with Dublin Castle. His period of office was dominated by successive Home Rule initiatives and battles at Westminster. Aberdeen's support for nationalist views meant the viceregal court was no longer the social centre of the unionist minority.

In his book *Champagne and Buckles: the Viceregal Court at Dublin Castle 1700-1922*, Joseph Robins quotes a member of the castle circle, Dublin architect P.L. Dickinson:

Social amenities were flung to the winds and the rag-tag and bobtail of Dublin went to court. After a few years of Aberdeen's term of office many people of breeding gave up all idea of going to the Castle, and social life in Dublin underwent an amazingly rapid decline …Without being a snob, it was no pleasure, and rather embarrassing, to meet the lady at dinner who had

41

Barton M'Guckin, a world famous tenor who was musical director of the exhibition.

Brendan J. Rogers, official organist to the exhibition.

IRISH INTERNATIONAL EXHIBITION, DUBLIN, 1907.
MAIN ENTRANCE   (Copyright)

A tram passes the Ballsbridge entrance to the exhibition. The red-bricked building on the extreme left is now Roly's Bistro. The entrance building stretched over to the corner of Elgin Road.

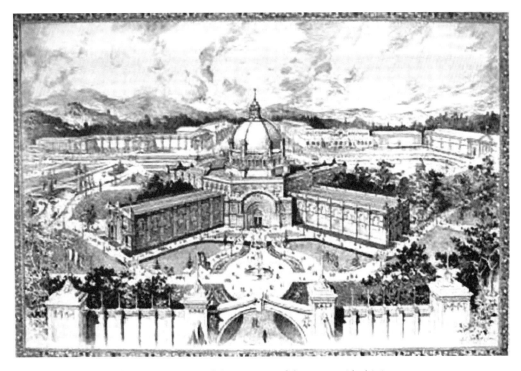

The *Illustrated London News* announced the opening of the event with this image.

measured you for your shirts the week before. As a result of this upsetting of values, social life in Dublin from the point of view of good breeding rapidly declined …

By the time of the St Patrick's Day Ball in 1907 there were fewer than sixty titled persons among the 2,000 guests – and one of them was Countess Constance Markievicz – which was a sure sign of how Aberdeen's Home Rule views had alienated him from loyalists.

Aberdeen was an avowed Liberal, and took a strong interest in the welfare of railway workers and small farmers in his native Scotland. With his wife Ishbel Marie Marjoribanks, he threw himself into Irish life and tirelessly promoted the health and general welfare of the Irish, as well as encouraging employment and culture. On his departure in 1915, *The Leader* commented that Aberdeen 'had opened everything in the city except the House of Parliament in College Green and the safe containing the Crown jewels'!

The viceroy was then presented by William Martin Murphy with a golden key to the building donated by the Corporation of Gold and Silversmiths of Ireland. Lord Aberdeen then commanded the Ulster King of Arms to declare the exhibition open, and the official then stepped forward and declared 'By command of his Excellency the Lord Lieutenant I proclaim this Exhibition open'. This was followed by a flourish of trumpets and a burst of applause. The six-month adventure had begun ….

A short concert commenced, with the *Hallelujah Chorus* followed by the Irish melody *When Through Life Unblest We Rove* and Elgar's march *Pomp and Circumstance*. As the VIPs left the orchestra played *St Patrick's Day* and two bars of *God Save the King*. The viceregal couple were taken on a short tour of the exhibits, being shown around the Gallery of Fine Arts by Alfred Temple and seeing some other highlights. The party left by the Morehampton Road entrance at 1.45 p.m.

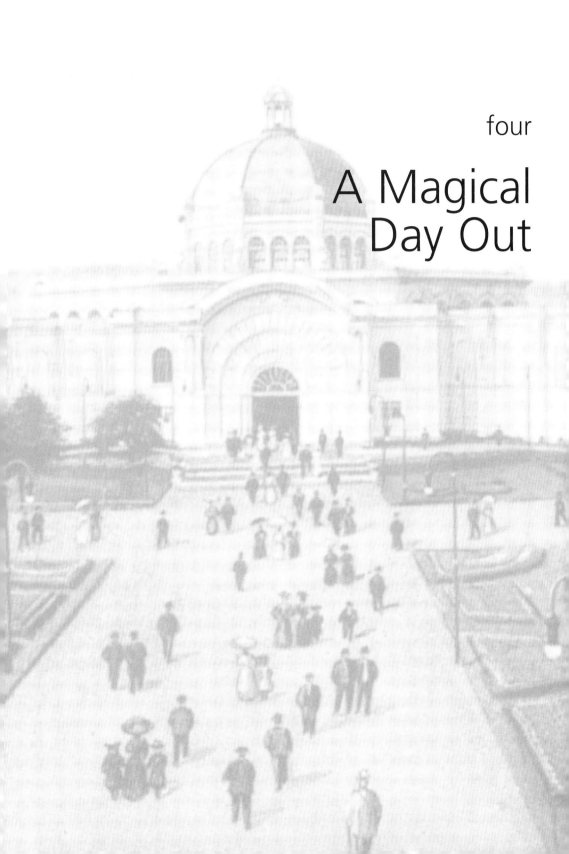

four

A Magical
Day Out

The exhibition was an instant success, with no fewer than 28,150 people going through the turnstiles the following Saturday. So what exactly was there to entice the citizens of Dublin to spend their hard-earned pennies? The exhibition certainly had plenty to see and do. Its enormous scale impressed the press who were given a sneak preview a week before the official opening: 'Initial feelings of wonderment deepen as the magnitude of the whole design and infinitude of its detail grows upon the understanding.' The exhibition occupied not only what is the modern Herbert Park, but also what is now an area covered in dozens of houses, bounded by Morehampton Road, Auburn Avenue, Home Villas and the Herbert Park central road, including Arranmore Road and Argyll Road.

There were entrances at Morehampton Road in Donnybrook, and at the confluence of Clyde Road, Elgin Road and Pembroke Road in Ballsbridge. Doors opened for the day at ten o'clock, and admission was secured for the price of one shilling or sixpence (if a child), paid at the turnstiles. Season tickets were priced at one guinea (approximately equal to €1.34) for adults and ten shillings and sixpence (67 cent) for children. A plaintive letter was sent to *The Irish Times* during the first weeks of the exhibition from a person signing themselves 'Industry and Justice'. The writer complained that the committee had 'entirely ignored the case of working men generally' and asked that a 10s 6d season ticket be introduced for artisans. 'We look upon the Exhibition as an educational medium', he wrote, 'and we want to go often; but a guinea is too much for a man who has to depend entirely on his weekly wage for a living.' He pointed out that working people could only spend a couple of hours there in the evening, 'whereas our more fortunate brethren, the leisured class, can spend the whole day there for the same figure'.

Whatever sum you paid, on entering you would have come into the main entrance hall, which contained kiosks selling the leading Dublin newspapers. It also contained a reproduction of the famous Celtic Cross of Monasterboice, a seventeen-feet-high sculpture carved out of a single piece of stone, which now resides in the National Museum in Kildare Street.

The entrance hall also featured kiosks for the principal railway and ferry companies, many of whom were key sponsors of the exhibition. Travelling for pleasure had come within reach of the middle classes of Dublin and there were several exhibits appealing to such customers: Thomas Cook's display consisted of a model of a Nile steamer, and one of a Dahabeah (Nile sailing boat). It also displayed models of Vesuvius, a Palestinian camp and two ancient Egyptian funeral boats. The ill-fated White Star Line (and its managers Ismay and Imrie) displayed models of their trans-Atlantic steamers, the *Cedric*, *Teutonic* and *Runic*, all of which were built by Harland and Wolff of Belfast, who had yet to build the liner that would send both companies' names down in infamy, the RMS *Titanic*.

You might have been accosted by one of the smartly uniformed boys selling programmes, a new edition of which was printed every day. This eight or twelve-page booklet, priced at one penny, detailed the various musical entertainments that would be staged that day, and there was usually quite a variety. A typical day would see an organ recital at 11 a.m., a recital in the concert hall from 12.30 p.m. till 3 p.m., a military band on the bandstand from 3 p.m. to 5.30 p.m., another concert from 5.30 p.m. to 8 p.m. and the return of the military band from 8 p.m. to 10.30 p.m. The exhibition closed at 11 p.m. each night. The programme also warned that 'visitors smoking or spitting in the Buildings will be liable to expulsion'. The *Freeman's Journal*

Right: A season ticket for the exhibition, which cost one guinea. The signature is that of James Shanks.

Below: The entrance hall contained several stands erected by the railway companies, who were among the investors and benefactors of the exhibition.

Above: Revington's Tweeds of Tralee took a stall in the Grand Central Palace. It sold Irish tweeds, homespun materials, fleece cloths and travelling rugs.

Left: One of the programmes which were printed daily and sold for a penny.

A guard of honour lines up outside the Grand Central Palace as a VIP party arrives.

Two little girls pose outside the Grand Central Palace.

IRISH INTERNATIONAL EXHIBITION, 1907.—VIEW FROM WATER CHUTE

The top of the water chute provided a good vantage point to view the exhibition.

IRISH INTERNATIONAL EXHIBITION, 1907.—GRAND CENTRAL PALACE (FRONT VIEW)

The Central Palace presented an impressive sight for visitors as they entered the grounds.

reported after a fortnight, that, 'In response to many requests, the Exhibition authorities have made arrangements under which children's perambulators will be admitted at various entrances'.

A favourite pastime at the time was the collecting of postcards, and special albums were sold to hold the many available from the exhibition, which were sold in kiosks at the entrance hall and around the grounds. The noted Dublin historian and cartophilist, F.E. Dixon, had a collection of 185 postcards, although there were many with just slight variations. The Dublin stationer James Tallon paid £350 for the rights to sell the postcards featuring views of the exhibition, although others such as Hely's and Lawrence's produced their own too. There were millions of these items produced and can still be bought cheaply today in antique shops or on internet auction sites.

In the centre of the main entrance hall was a remarkable scale model of the Battle of Waterloo, built in Dublin by Captain William Siborne some seventy years before. Siborne had joined the British Army in 1813 and was posted to France. He had a keen interest in the Battle of Waterloo, stirred by conversations with veterans of the battle. He also developed a skill at topography and wrote books on the subject. In 1830, Lord 'Daddy' Hill, commander-in-chief of the British Army, commissioned Siborne to make a model of the Battle of Waterloo, which would be dedicated to the Duke of Wellington, by then Prime Minister. Siborne spent many months in Belgium surveying the battlefield and commenced building his project.

Siborne ran into political difficulties early in the project. The government changed and when he submitted a bill for expenses he was told that no record existed of his commission. After weeks of toing and froing Siborne received the expenses he had incurred to date, but was

A small part of William Siborne's New Model of the Battle of Waterloo.

IRISH INTERNATIONAL EXHIBITION, 1907—CONCERT HALL

The Concert Hall on a slow day.

informed that no more funding would be forthcoming for his model. Siborne continued to, unsuccessfully, lobby Earl Gray's government for the money he had promised to tradesmen and craftsmen for work done. He continued to work on the model at his own expense, and at some stage in this he was transferred to Dublin. A whip-round of officers who served at Waterloo was organised and they each contributed at least £20.

In October 1836, Siborne sent the Duke a copy of the final plan. Wellington wrote a memo endorsing it, but indicated that he could not really remember with any accuracy where any of the troops were. Siborne became embroiled in controversy some years later as the positions given by him to the Prussians conflicted with the Duke's account. Wellington had played down the role of his Prussian allies in the battle to maximise his own share of the glory. Siborne had read the Prussian authorities on the battle and corresponded with the Prussian general staff and cross-checked their comments with those of the French. However, Siborne could not take up Wellington's invitation to come to see him in England. He simply could not pay for the trip as all his funds were being spent on the construction of the model. He took out bank loans set against his life assurance and finally, in 1838 completed his marathon project. It went on display in October that year in the Egyptian Hall in Piccadilly and later went on tour around Britain. It was a massive success, with more than 100,000 members of the public paying £5,000 to see the enormous model. However, Siborne seemed to have struck a poor deal with the promoters and his cut did not cover the debts of £3,000 he had incurred. He again petitioned the authorities for assistance but the controversy over the Prussians seems to have been his downfall.

In September 1841 he decided to sell the model, first approaching the Royal Dublin Society who he hoped would appreciate the fine Irish craftsmanship on display. Siborne finally made some money when he wrote *The History of the Campaign in France and Belgium in 1815*, the project

The bandstand was a popular attraction. The Palace Restaurant is behind on the right. Beyond that are tea rooms and the Canadian Pavilion.

Looking up Royal Avenue from the Morehampton Road entrance. The Canadian Pavilion is on the left.

The workers on the left, sporting jerseys with 'IIE' emblazoned upon them, recovered the boats after use and set them up for new customers.

he had abandoned in 1830 in favour of the model. Siborne later built a larger scale model of part of the battlefield, The New Model. The models went on tour again, including a year-long exhibition in Berlin, but money was still an issue and Siborne attempted to sell shares in his ventures, but he died in 1849 before he could take up the sums offered.

In 1850 the original model was purchased by the United Service Institution for just over £2,000, and it went on permanent display in its museum where it remained until 1962 when it was broken down into its thirty-nine parts and sent to the Royal Military Academy, Sandhurst, for storage. There it remained until 1975 when it was inspected by a number of specialists and, under expert supervision, restored to its former glory. Since 1990 the model has been on display at the National Army Museum in London. The New Model was displayed in Germany in 1848 and sent to Dublin in 1851, where it appears to have gone into storage in an ironworks. After the Irish International Exhibition it again disappeared from view before it was discovered in the attic of Mrs Barrington-Malone in south County Dublin. It was repaired and restored and is now on display at the Royal Armouries in Leeds.

The New Model, which showed Uxbridge's great cavalry charge made between 1 p.m. and 2 p.m., covered an area of battle 1,200 yards long by 530 yards wide (on a scale of 15 feet to 1 inch, which means the model measured about 66 yards x 30 yards). In Dublin it was placed in the middle of the main entrance hall as it was too large for the Fine Art Gallery.

As the visitor emerged from the entrance hall he would have been confronted by a wondrous sight. All around were bright white structures designed in Italian Renaissance style, colourful lawns and flowerbeds. Footpaths led to, on the left, the bandstand and water chute, or, on the right, the Palace of Industries. Straight ahead was the largest of the buildings, the magnificent Central Palace, which also served as the musical centre of the exhibition. Music was an important element

As a boat splashes into the lake on the right of the picture; the staff ride another up the track to the top of the Canadian water chute where eager punters wait.

The looks of delight are obvious as this family begins its thrilling descent, although the young boy on the left seems slightly nervous.

Spectators lined the banks to watch the craft's progress down and around the pond.

of the offering, and it came under the auspices of Musical Director Barton M'Guckin, a famous Irish tenor. M'Guckin was born in Dublin 1852 and studied in Armagh, Dublin and Milan. He was the first to sing the role of *Othello* in English in England and also performed in the United States. He made his first recording in 1883. M'Guckin took control of the state ceremonials at the opening and closing ceremonies, for which he was paid tribute by the committee who wrote that his 'capacity as a teacher and organiser was splendidly attested under many difficulties throughout his tenure of the office he filled so efficiently and with so much credit to himself'.

Bands performed in the Central Palace and on the bandstand, while there was an organ in the Concert Hall and ballad concerts in the Village Hall. Thirty-two different bands, mostly military, were engaged by the organisers. The band of the Grenadier Guards were the most expensive, costing 300 guineas a week plus travelling expenses of £84. The 87th Royal Irish Fusiliers were a far cheaper option and were hired for seven and a half weeks at £100 a week. Cheaper still were the 4th Dublin Fusiliers (£38 10s a week, and no travelling expenses). There were many individual entertainers – the English singer and novelist George *(Diary of a Nobody)* Grossmith among them – while some of the groups have names that sound suspiciously like 1960s pop bands: The Wheelers, The Motorists and The Tatlers.

The concert hall proved to be highly popular during the exhibition. It was used daily and nightly, under the auspices of the official organist, Brendan J. Rogers. There were complaints that the noise in the adjoining halls drowned out the music, and a F.H. de L. Roper of Leeson Park wrote to the newspapers suggesting that a sand floor be laid on the Central Hall to muffle the 'continual noises caused by people passing to and fro'.

In addition to the musical performances, a succession of vaudeville, or variety, entertainments were staged there. With the international nature of the exhibition, many of these were foreign

IRISH INTERNATIONAL EXHIBITION, 1907.
COMING UNDER BRIDGE FROM WATER CHUTE

Momentum carried the boat under two bridges and around the little islands.

Refreshments were an important element of the exhibition's programme. This was the Popular Restaurant, one of four restaurants on the site.

acts, with several conjurors, rope-walkers and dancers. A gymnastic display by boys of the Royal Hibernian Military School took place on 6 July. Ten days later the constabulary band performed *Yeoman of the Guard*. The exhibition record listed thirty-two bands and orchestras that performed, with the nineteen weeks of the Grandpierre Orchestra the longest run by far. Others who had lengthy runs were the band of the Royal Irish Fusiliers (the Faugh-a-Ballaghs) who lasted seven and a half weeks, Herr Kandt's Orchestra (six weeks) and Herr Von Leer's Casino Orchestra (four weeks). Some groups were given just one day to show off their talents, including the Dublin Total Abstinence Working Men's Band (fee: £5), the Sarsfield Band from Limerick (who waived their fee but claimed £11 3s in expenses) and the York Street Workman's Band. Expenditure on bands and orchestras, including travel, was £11,220, and other expenses connected with the musical entertainment were £6,077. Receipts from the music totalled £26,258, producing a surplus of £9,000.

From the Central Palace the visitor might have headed towards the commotion caused by the shrieks of laughter of the customers of the Canadian water chute. This, of all the features in the exhibition, was remembered with affection many years later by those who rode upon it. The water chute stood at the Ballsbridge end of the pond, which was specially constructed for the exhibition. The chute consisted of a tall tower standing about ninety feet high with a ramp, bearing two sets of rails, leading down into the pond. Having paid a sixpence, people would climb the tower and enter a small boat with room for eight people and a steersman. We can only imagine the excitement as the craft slid faster and faster down the ramp before hitting the water and then skimming across the surface to travel under two bridges before coming to a halt at the far end of the pond, some sixty yards distant. During the six months of the exhibition the chute, which cost £3,000 to erect, took in £7,000, making it the second most profitable venture.

On 29 June *The Irish Times* reported what was headlined as 'A Ludicrous Incident'. Students of Trinity commandeered two boats after they had descended the chute and 'took over' one of the islands in the pond. The jape went awry and as the newspaper reported, 'to regain terra firma many got very wet', as one of the pirated craft overturned into the pond, drenching the hapless buccaneers.

As the visitor continued southwards from the pond, to where the Gaelic football and soccer pitches now stand, he or she would come across the Home Industries section, which comprised a central building and several smaller constructions. In many ways this was the most important section, certainly in terms of the stated aims of the exhibition committee, and it was thus decided to give free spaces to rural industries which could not afford to pay. Industries were selected which would be 'creditable to Ireland and themselves' and 'would be able to make headway, if so assisted'. The Home Industries section had 177 entries, with many manufacturers of linen, lace, tweeds, carpets, crochet and embroidery. The Arts and Crafts subsection featured dozens of examples of enamel work, jewellery, leather work and book-binding. This Home Industries Pavilion was presided over by the Countess of Aberdeen who had progressive views. The committee also resolved to include as far as possible all branches of rural economy, and to feature working exhibits of successful industries.

A special *Handbook of Irish Rural Life and Industy* with suggestions for the future, by the committee secretary W.T.M. McCarthy-Filgate, was printed. Its 360 pages, plus advertisements, cost 3s 6d. The foreword, by Lady Aberdeen, exhorted its readers, 'May this book fulfill its mission of inciting readers to *do* as well as to *think*.' Much of the book can be seen as a source book for information about what was being done to prepare Ireland for Home Rule, and what could be learned from other countries. There were more than fifty articles therein, including practical guides to bee-keeping, flax making, tobacco, embroidery, lace, gloves, straw hats, curtains and carpets. A member of the Addis family wrote about toothbrush manufacturing, while P.W. Joyce

Patrons of the helter skelter plunged fifty feet to earth in just nine seconds.

Snacks were available from the Oxo and Lemco stalls. This was situated next to the water chute.

The Indian Theatre was a well-attended sideshow.

Entrance to the Somali Village at the south-western corner of the exhibition.

wrote on 'Ancient Irish Industries and Irish Folklore'. Artist Dermod O'Brien wrote about Irish dancing, while Lady Dudley outlined her scheme for district nurses.

All this information and entertainment must have been tiring, so the visitor would need an invigorating cup of tea, which was available in kiosks and tea shops throughout the grounds. The Lipton Tea Pavilion did good business, although it is not recorded whether they sold the anticipated two million cups. If they did, the 'Cingalese' (presumably Singhalese) boys who acted as waiters would have been exhausted.

The corner of the park nearest to Donnybrook village was set aside for sideshows and amusements. Among these was a 'Helter Skelter Lighthouse' (flying the American flag, the slide rose fifty feet above the ground and promised to return you to earth in nine seconds, for twopence), a Switchback Railway, Indian Jugglers (Ebrahim Sahib's Fakirs), a Crystal Maze (distorting mirrors), a Shooting Jungle (life-like representations of animals in their natural habitats) and the Rivers of Ireland (travellers sailed through a tunnel in a small boat as images of the rivers were displayed). Educational sideshows included beehives and ants' nests, which were exposed and magnified. Miss Grace Burns explained what was going on but receipts came to just £400 over the six-month run.

Several families of Somalians were housed in the Somali Village exhibit, which replicated their own dwellings back in Africa. There they carried out their daily tasks and made craft items which they sold. *The Irish Times* reported on 27 May that 'the Somali potter was of a cheery temperament and lightened his toil with the wild songs of his native land'. They were also described as 'good-natured, dark, but not unthreatening'.

The newspapers also reported that rumours of ill-health among the Africans were unfounded:

Dr G. Preston-Ball, who visits the Village twice daily, certifies that, with the exception of slight colds, which a few have contracted on account of the severe weather, the Somalis are in

Above: The Africans sold the crafts they produced at this little stall. The Somali potter was 'of cheery temperament' according to *The Irish Times.*

Left: Some warriors from Somaliland.

Above: The Somali men in traditional dress.

Right: The women of the Somali Village line up for the cameraman.

Irish International Exhibition Dublin 1907
The Somali Village

The Africans must have been an exotic addition to the Irish summer.

good health. There have been no deaths, and no case of infectious diseases. The man with the wounded arm is now convalescent …

The Irish Times reported that they 'by no means relish the climate of the country, though taking singularly little precaution to defend themselves against it'. Some days later the newspaper remarked that although the Somalis had been provided with flannel clothing, 'their individual wishes have to be respected in regard to clothing, as well as in other respects, as they are under free contracts'.

A minor controversy flared up when one of the Somali children was 'kidnapped', but returned unharmed. It turned out to be a prank by the Dublin eccentric William 'The Bird' Flanagan. Flanagan, who attracted his nickname when his chicken costume failed to win a fancy dress event and he pretended to lay an egg in front of the judges, was celebrated for his practical jokes, including bringing a corpse into the snug in Neary's Bar, and riding a horse into the bar of the Gresham Hotel. When the barman pointed out that it was past closing time, the Bird exclaimed 'The drink isn't for me, it's for the horse!'

Such tribal sideshows were popular in Edwardian Britain; a Somali village had been a hit at the Bradford Exhibition in 1904, while Edinburgh had a village inhabited by 100 Senegalese. Edinburgh originally intended to hold an International Exhibition to mark the bicentenary of the Union of Scotland and England in 1907 but Dublin had already earmarked that year for its own exhibition. Edinburgh, instead, held its Scottish National Exhibition, which opened on 1 May 1908 at Saughton Park. Its organisers clearly studied the Herbert Park model as its attractions also included a switchback railway, a helter skelter and water chute! Several of these exhibits were moved to a permanent site at Portobello in the city, but the Senegalese were unable to stay in Edinburgh following the exhibition, so some Somalis were recruited in their place.

The Italian terrace, with an inset of Alfred Temple, curator of the Fine Arts Section.

The interest in the village and its inhabitants in Dublin was such that the takings of £9,600 were by far the highest of the sideshows, outstripping even the water chute. The folk memory of the Africans lived on for many years in one corner of Dublin. A hillside development of houses in Howth was built at this time and was known affectionately as 'the Somali Village'.

The promoters of the Somalis had a good deal, being obliged to hand over just 25 per cent of its takings to the organisers. The Indian Theatre paid one-third of its income of £2,350 while Toft's Amusements stumped up half of the £1,400 they took in on the hobby horses and swingboats. While these attractions were operated on a concession basis, the exhibition installed the water chute itself (£4,000 clear profit), as well as the helter skelter (£2,000). One mystifying concession was the 'Hat Renovating Percentage' which earned £5 1s 5d.

As the visitor headed west he would have come across the 33,000 square foot Palace of Fine Arts, which was divided into seven compartments and came under the direction of Sir Walter Armstrong, director of the National Gallery of Ireland, who curated works by Irish artists, and Alfred Temple, director of the Guildhall Gallery in London. Temple explained his aims in an article in the *Art Journal* in July 1907:

> … a full display of the oil painting and water colour art of the British School in recent years, a broad representation of British sculpture, of miniature painting and black and white work, and to provide for a notable exhibition of works in oil by some of the more prominent painters in France, Spain, Holland, Belgium, Germany and other foreign countries.

Temple won much praise for the breadth and quality of the works he secured, and his decision to include only works from the previous half-century ensured a vibrant, living exhibition.

Inside the Fine Arts Palace, with an inset of Colonel Courteney CB DL, who was Chairman of the Historical and Educational Committee.

The Fine Art Palace hosted several independent exhibitions. It contained nearly 1,500 paintings, sculptures, prints and drawings, as well as more than 400 photographs. The works included a series of portraits by John Butler Yeats of his son W.B. Yeats, John Millington Synge and George Moore among others. There were sixteen paintings by Charles Shannon, the most by any individual, and other Irish artists displayed included William Orpen, John Lavery, Walter Osborne and Nathaniel Hone. Also on show was 'Portrait of an Officer' by Count Casimir Dunin-Markiewicz, husband of Constance Gore-Booth.

Among the most popular exhibits were thirteen works by Walter Osborne, including 'The Thornbush' (1894), of which Professor Thomas Bodkin wrote in 1920: 'This picture is regarded by many as Osborne's masterpiece. I cannot think of any landscape by which he might be more fitly represented.' A reproduction of this painting was included in the souvenir *Folio of Famous Pictures* produced by the exhibition. 'The Thornbush' has changed hands several times over the last century, the most recent being in November 2006 when it sold at Whyte's Auction House in Dublin for €400,000.

Many important galleries and individuals sent works, including the Tsar of Russia, who lent an enormous, gruesome work by Alexander Borisoff which showed the last to die of a party of marooned Arctic hunters. The subject is being devoured by an Arctic fox. King Edward VII lent Lady Butler's Crimean War scene 'The Roll Call'. 'A Highland Scene near Dalmally' by the celebrated Myles Birket Foster was also shown, as were 'The Execution of Marshal Ney' by J.L. Gerome, 'The Depths of the Sea' by Sir E. Burne-Jones and 'The Last Moments of Raphael' by Henry O'Neil. Other artists who had works on show included the popular Pre-Raphaelites Ford Madox Brown, Dante Gabriel Rossetti, and John Everett Millais. The art exhibitions were popular and inspirational. The great Irish artist

'The Thornbush' by Walter Osborne, which was hung at the exhibition. It sold in 2006 for €400,000.

'The Execution of Marshal Ney' by J.L. Gerome.

There was a fine display of Irish silverware in the Fine Arts Pavilion. These silver potato rings were lent by Colonel Claude Cane.

Harry Clarke recalled how he was first exposed to the works of Aubrey Beardsley at the Irish International Exhibition. A notable exhibitor in the sculpture section was twenty-six-year-old Willie Pearse, only brother of Padraig. Willie had a modest degree of artistic talent and between 1906 and 1913 he also exhibited work at the Royal Hibernian Academy and the *Oireachtas* exhibitions.

The Fine Arts Palace also housed the Historical Collection, which was curated by Colonel Arthur Courteney CB DL, who 'devoted many months of daily and nightly labour, toiling, in his capacity of Honorary Secretary of the Historical Committee, with a zeal far surpassing that of any paid official', according to the official record. The Irish Historical Collection was a bizarre melange of 1,243 artifacts, with strong representation of glass and silverware. Lenders included the Ouzel Galley Society (the Boatswain's whistle and the club's medal) and the Goldsmith's Guild (their charter and plates of punchmarks). The notorious Hell Fire Club's punchbowl was on display, as well as its presumably overactive corkscrew. Other interesting pieces included the trowel used to lay the foundation stone of the O'Connell Monument, and the Liberator's own gold watch and umbrella. A mortuary locket containing the hair of Queen Mary, wife of George III was on show, as was the silver spade and bog oak barrow presented to Charles Stuart Parnell at the opening of the Ennis railway. The infant clothes worn by Lord Edward Fitzgerald were exhibited next to the gloves left behind at Lismullen by King William. Also included was a huge collection of pieces of antique Irish Silver, the autograph and seal of Dean Swift, and his snuff box, an extensive collection of memorabilia to do with the Irish Volunteers Militia founded in 1779, the fifteenth-century *Book of Lismore*, a pledge card for Father Mathew's temperance movement, Daniel O'Connell's Clare election certificate 1828 ('framed in part of the outer coffin in which his remains were brought from Genoa in 1847'), the mace of the Irish House

View from the dome over the pond to the Home Industries Pavilion. The tower of St Mary's Church, Simmonscourt Road, can be seen behind the pavilion.

of Commons, the uniform Henry Joy McCracken wore at the Battle of Antrim and the stirrups the Duc de Schomberg wore at the Battle of the Boyne. The eccentric mixture was probably the result of the collection being put together from many donors and lenders, including Trinity College, the Belfast Corporation, the Royal Irish Academy, and the Victoria and Albert Museum. One of the most popular exhibits was a dug-out canoe from early times, now on display in the National Museum in Kildare Street.

In the smallest room of the palace was placed a fascinating collection of no fewer than 400 Napoleonic relics lent by Professor T.H. Teegan and Mr N. Bonaparte-Wyse. Many of these artifacts are now on show in the Waterford Museum of Treasures, lent by the Bonaparte-Wyse family. It had been intended that Siborne's scale model of the Battle of Waterloo would reside in the Palace of Fine Arts but it was far too large for the available space.

The committee was particularly delighted with the efforts of Alfred Temple, and as the exhibition's run drew to a close they decided to present him with a token of appreciation. West's of College Green made a replica of a George II silver urn of Dublin manufacture, while his wife was presented with a diamond ornament. Temple paid tribute to those who assisted him, particularly Colonel Courteney and sculptor George Frampton. He also reported that he:

> … shall not easily forget the observation which was made in my hearing by His Majesty the King to His Excellency the Lord Lieutenant, when I had the honour of conducting His Majesty and Queen Alexandra through the British and Continental Section. His Majesty said – 'I had not expected to see such a collection in Dublin. If my time is short, I will go more quickly; but I must see it all'.

The flowerbeds and lawns that led up to the Home Industries Pavilion.

Temple finished by saying:

> I have always felt an interest in the Irish people, and this interest has grown now to be one almost of affection, and it makes me think that, after all, the only thing which really divides England from this beautiful and energetic isle is the narrow strip of water, which can be traversed in a couple of hours.

Temple was knighted in 1920 and died, aged seventy-nine, in 1928.

Outside the art gallery and the industries hall were two attractive fountains, which, after 16 July, were illuminated at night. The gallery itself was decorated at night by 12,000 fairy lights.

The longest building was that occupied by the Palace of Mechanical Arts which stretched 300 yards from the back wall of the modern Herbert Park up to the perimeter at Morehampton Road. This imposing edifice contained examples of heavy machinery and the many uses of electricity. There were large-scale models of ocean liners, printing presses and a model, fully-functioning bakery.

The visitor had then reached the furthest point in the exhibition from the Ballsbridge entrance. He could then turn and visit three buildings along the northern side of the central road. These were the Alliance Gas Company Pavilion, the Tudor-style Canadian Pavilion and a teashop.

The Canadian government sponsored a whole pavilion, which was opened some days after the exhibition opened. It carried a large poster inside the entrance which read:

> CAUTION: Whilst reading matter in this building is based on facts, do not be influenced by it. Canada wants settlers; but she does not want people who are satisfied with their present conditions to leave their native land.

The Palace of Fine Arts. The pergola that was later erected in Herbert Park follows the line of the façade of this building.

Looking up the pond from the Donnybrook end towards the water chute.

Lady attendants on the Indian stall of Ardeshir & Co. It displayed Indian works of art. To the right are some examples of Italian sculpture.

The Canadian authorities pledged that they would welcome settlers 'with open arms' to the vast dominion, and would not subject them 'to an alien tax of two dollars per head'. The Canadian representative became embroiled in controversy later in the summer when he declared that 'the Jews in Canada could not be viewed as permanent settlers'.

Its exhibits were divided into seven sections: agriculture, fruit culture, products of the forest, economic minerals, dairy and food produce, fisheries, and fauna. The latter was very popular, displaying in a large area 'magnificent specimens of a large variety of animals, all indigenous to the country'. On show were the polar bear, musk ox, buffalo, moose, caribou, wapiti, red deer, elk, grizzly bear, black bear, beaver, racoon, fox, mink, marten, badger, and wolf, as well as a large selection of birds.

All this activity might have sparked hunger and thirst in the visitor. Several restaurants were built to cater for the large crowds that continued to attend all summer, the largest of which was the Palace Restaurant beside the concert hall. A vegetarian restaurant was another novel feature.

There was a competition to find the best type of worker's cottage, with the winner, which sold for £135, being a type still to be seen in the city and county. A builder called William Pickering set up a stall on which he displayed models of the homes he could build, which proved a success for his firm. Examples can be seen today at Park Drive, Ranelagh. A house called Milverton in Herbert Park was built as a show house by the top builders of the day, Cramptons. It sold again in 2005 for more than €8 million. The exhibition also had fully built examples of a village hall and a village hospital which cost just £285 to erect.

The ornamental Italian sculpture of Signor Bazzanti of Florence. There were some complaints that the Italian sculptor's work was overpriced.

Inside the Palace of Industries, with the leading Dublin department store Clerys on the right.

The vast pavilion that housed the Mechanical Arts exhibits. This pavilion provided electric light and heat for the exhibition. Gas was also provided from a separate structure across the Royal Avenue.

Next along was the French Pavilion, and on what is now a bowling green stood the Palace of Industries, which was also occupied by many of the trade exhibitors who paid almost £23,000 for the space they occupied. There were 538 Irish exhibitors, 278 from France, 187 from Britain and 26 from Italy. There were also a handful from Japan, Holland, Germany and Belgium, as well as one each from Hungary, Armenia and Argentina, bringing the total to 1,044. In addition to these, there were exhibits gathered by the Governor-General of Algeria, the Government of the Dominion of New Zealand, and the Agent-General for the Cape of Good Hope, showcasing a large variety of products from Algeria, New Zealand and South Africa.

The exhibitors in the Irish Industries section included manufacturers of stained glass ('Brian Boru addressing his troops on the morning of the Battle of Clontarf' by James Watson & Co, Youghal) and baby cars (The Castlecomer Perambulator Works and Basket Industry). Although the exhibition is now a century adrift in memory, a large number of concerns that took an active part in the activities still exist in Dublin today, or did so until recent years. Among those who exhibited were some well known Grafton Street landmarks including Thomas Cook travel agents, Switzers; J.M. Barnardo, furrier; Kapp & Peterson, tobacconist; and Messrs Brown, Thomas & Co. Other familiar names include Pigott's musical instruments; Dockrell's builders' providers; Macardle's brewery, Dundalk; Singer sewing machine company; Elvery's sporting goods; Elephant House; Winstanley's boots and shoes; Callaghan's equestrian equipment, Dame Street; McBirney's haberdashery, Aston Quay; Hayes, Conyngham and Robinson, pharmacists; Hamilton, Long and Co., pharmacists; Eason and Son, booksellers; Varian brushes; Paterson matches; The Ringsend Bottle Company; Hely's printers; Gallaher tobacco, Belfast; J.S. Fry confectioners; Lemon and Son, confectioners; W & R Jacob, biscuits; John Jameson & Son, distillers; Crosse & Blackwell, preserved provisions, Cork; Cleeve Bros,

The Right Hon.
Lord Castletown. K.P.

Col Sir John Arnott. Bart KP.

The Right Hon Lord Viscount Iveagh. K.P.

Sir Wᵐ J. Goulding. Bart. D.L.

Sir John Nutting
Bart. D.L.

Five Knights of the Exhibition: these titled gentlemen were vice-presidents and members of the
Executive Council. The central figure, Lord Iveagh, did not take an active role in the exhibition, but
stumped up a guarantee for £10,000.

The colony of New Zealand rented a small area to exhibit its wares and attractions. There was even a refrigerated chamber holding examples of sheep, pork and poultry.

confectioners, Limerick; Tyler's footwear; John G. Rathborne, candles; and Denny, Limerick, producer of bacon, hams and lard.

The official *Record of the Exhibition* boasted that the arrangement of the raw and manufactured products shown at Herbert Park 'were not in accordance with a definite system of classification. The result was that monotony was, to a large extent, avoided', which sounds like a justification-after-the-fact for a poorly organised layout!

The visitor's eccentric progress around the grounds continued with the Celtic Court, the Model Dairy and the Lipton Pavilion. The Celtic Court was a popular meeting place, and its central feature was a colossal statue called *Erin* by Messrs Wurshing and Trautner, modellers and sculptors in the nearby village of Ranelagh. Next to this, shielded from delicate eyes, was an area leading onto Clyde Lane where deliveries were made to storerooms and larders, and the exhibition staff were quartered.

The visitor would then return to the entrance hall, where he might enjoy tea in another of the restaurants before picking up some postcards and other souvenirs and then departing. It must have been a memorable day for those who attended. A film of the activities was made on 9 May, but has been lost in the mists of time. On that day 20,150 people paid threepence, sixpence and one shilling to gain admission. The various halls and sideshows were not all open from the start; they seem to have been phased in over the following weeks to encourage publicity but all were in full swing by 10 July, when some important visitors arrived from London.

The Chivers tea shop.

The bridge over the pond with the Grand Central Palace behind.

Women working, making McClintock's soap at the exhibition.

The sideshows in the corner of Herbert Park near Donnybrook which is now partly occupied by a soccer pitch. The switchback railway can be seen on the right.

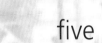

The King, he came to call on us

Lord Aberdeen had returned to Ballsbridge on Saturday 1 June to open the Home Industries section. Heavy rain fell all day, so the ceremony had to be moved indoors from the village green. Lady Aberdeen arrived at 3 p.m. and mounted the dais on the green. She was welcomed by the Revd P.J. Dowling who asserted that 'for the first time on Irish soil, we see a most attractive feature of a great International Exhibition – the display of those industries which are gradually assuming such importance in the life of every people'. He also paid tribute to 'all who are working for the betterment of their countryman' who would find that at the exhibition they could 'behold ideas to work towards, in industries, housing, developing the recreative side of country life, and bringing the advantages of modern hygiene to the bedside of the sick'.

Lady Aberdeen replied by congratulating the spirit behind the exhibition, and pointing to the exhibits of the 'supplemental industries' which, she said, 'cannot fail to have a great influence on the lives and characters of those who cultivate them, training them in diverse ways, and imbuing them with new hopes and ambitions, as they begin to realise the results of their labours'.

Her own passion for improving the health of the poor was well known, and she spoke at length about how the exhibition would help this:

> Look at our little emergency hospital … and consider the comfort and help that such an institution could be in outlying parts of Ireland, allowing the district nurses to be sent out in couples, instead of singly as at present, and giving the medical men of the district the opportunity of having their serious cases under observation and carefully nursed.

It fell on Lady Aberdeen, as president of the Home Industries section, to welcome her husband to the exhibition hall. She too was presented with a golden key, this one made and donated by West's jewellers of College Green. She joked that she would 'lend' it to her husband before taking him on a tour of the buildings.

Moving on from the Home Industries hall, the party headed for the Palace of Fine Arts but on their way they were interrupted by a noisy outburst from the Somali Village, '… they were greeted by the dusky inhabitants of that settlement in barbaric but friendly fashion'. The men of the party were in full war attire, carrying their swords, spears and shields, and, as the viceregal procession approached, they brandished and clashed these accoutrements, uttering wild cries of applause and welcome. On coming within speaking distance, Lord Aberdeen, addressing the Somali Chief, expressed his own and Lady Aberdeen's appreciation of the compliment thus paid them, and their regret that lack of knowledge of the Somali language prevented them from doing so in their own tongue. His Excellency added, however, that he had on his staff a distinguished officer fully conversant with their dialect, whom he would ask to tell them what he had said.

> Captain the Hon A Hore-Ruthven VC, Aide-de-Camp, translated His Excellency's remarks for the benefit of the dusky warriors, and the chief replied briefly in the same language … the Somali indulged in another series of whoops, which was their nearest approach to cheering, and as the Vice-Regal party drove away bowing and smiling, the chief urged his followers to another series of yells, which was given with energy and much brandishing of weapons.

THE ROYAL PROCESSION LEAVING KINGSTOWN FOR THE IRISH INTERNATIONAL EXHIBITION *[D'Ar*

The Earl and Countess of Aberdeen drove in the first carriage followed by the Royal Equipage with Their Majesties the King and Queen.

The Royal party drive up the hill from the quay in Kingstown (Dun Laoghaire) where they arrived in the Royal Yacht. The viceroy and his wife are in the carriage nearest the camera.

Above, left and right: King Edward VII and his queen, Alexandra of Denmark. 'Bertie' was born in 1841, but was almost sixty when he acceded to the throne on the death of his mother Queen Victoria. He died less than three years after his visit to Dublin.

The royal carriage arrives at the exhibition.

IRISH INTERNATIONAL EXHIBITION, DUBLIN, 1907.—ARRIVAL OF THE KING AND QUEEN
(Copyright)

The party drive past the Fine Arts Pavilion to the Grand Central Palace.

The procession drives along a route lined by members of the armed forces.

The King and Queen walking to the concert hall for the ceremony.

IRISH INTERNATIONAL EXHIBITION.

Visit of Their Majesties the King and Queen, 10th July, 1907.

CHOIR & ORCHESTRA PASS.

ADMIT ONE.

James Shanks

Chief Executive Officer.

{SEE OVER.]

Admission ticket issued to one of the musicians for the Royal visit.

No. 2

ROYAL  VISIT.

ADMIT BEARER

to Special Enclosure at Kingstown Railway Station on Wednesday, 10th July, 1907.

By Order of the Directors,

M. F. KEOGH,
Secretary.

THIS CARD TO BE PRODUCED.

Invitation to the special enclosure at the arrival of the Royals in Kingstown, issued by the Dublin and South Eastern railway company.

The formal procession arrives at the hall, led by the Marquess of Ormonde, with James Shanks (left) and William Martin Murphy (right) following. Behind them are the King (doffing his hat), Queen and Lord Aberdeen.

The translator, Alexander Hore-Ruthven, later had a distinguished career as a soldier in France and Gallipoli, and as a diplomat, helping soothe the tensions between Britain and Australia over the fractious 'Bodyline' cricket series.

The next port of call for the viceregal party was to the Italian section, where they were greeted by Count Lorenzo Salazar, the consul. Salazar had invited more than a thousand guests who lined up to meet the Aberdeens and enjoyed the fare of the Palace Restaurant.

The Lord Lieutenant was back again on Saturday 29 June, to open the French Pavilion on the invitation of the Consul for France, Monsieur Lefeuvre Meaulle. Their handsome building had been designed by Parisian architect M. de Montarnai and was packed with typical produce including wines, ciders, *eaux-de-vie*, ceramics, furniture, and liqueurs.

Their Excellencies were greeted, in French, by Leon Barbier, President of the *Comite des Expositions de l'Etranger*, and presented with a French fan. The tone of the speeches was extremely cordial, with the *Entente Cordiale* of 1904 considerably warming Britain's relationship with France. Monsieur Barbier insisted that the King was 'as popular in France as in England and Ireland', while Aberdeen agreed that the King was 'a warm and assured friend of France, and therefore of the head of the French Republic'. He also pointed out that while the *Entente Cordiale* was a recent event, 'in Ireland it was a matter of history and of long duration. Now their English friends are following their example and recognising its beneficence'.

King Edward VII and his Queen, Alexandra, and their entourage, which included their daughter Princess Victoria, arrived at 8 a.m. on 10 July in Kingstown, now Dun Laoghaire. They did not disembark from the Royal Yacht until Lord and Lady Aberdeen arrived to

The Canadian Pavilion at the Donnybrook end.

greet them at 11 a.m. and then travelled by open carriage to the showgrounds along roads hung with bunting and banners. The five and a half mile journey from the Victoria Wharf to Ballsbridge took them along Crofton Road, Dunleary Road, Longford Terrace, Clifton Place, Monkstown Road, Blackrock Road, Booterstown, Merrion Road, Ailesbury Road, past Donnybrook Fair Green into Donnybrook, and along Morehampton Road to the exhibition entrance. They were accompanied on their journey through the suburbs by mounted Hussars and Cameron Highlanders. There was some excitement caused by the progress of two empty carriages piloted by two Knights of the Whip. They were followed at a canter by two mounted police which, according to *The Irish Times*, 'would have done credit to Orby', the latter being the celebrated Irish racehorse who had won the Epsom Derby a fortnight before. Whether these empty carriages were concocted as a security measure to act as a decoy for the main procession is not known.

Over the long day their majesties had to undergo the reciting of loyal addresses of welcome from the various urban district councils such as Kingstown, Dalkey, Blackrock and Pembroke, and many, many others. In response to the welcome from the Kingstown Council, the King pointed to that 'unabated interest' which his Queen took 'in Irish Cottage Industries, as in everything that relates to the well-being of our Irish people'.

They arrived at the exhibition at about 1.10 p.m., with the *Irish Independent* describing that 'all along Merrion, Ailesbury Road, Donnybrook Road, through the village, and up to the gates of the Exhibition the cheering travelled, growing in volume as the crowds increased, and finally swelling into a magnificent, sustained outburst of welcome as their Majesties reached the entrance'. According to the official report, 'The demonstration was a convincing proof of the feelings of affection entertained by the citizens of Dublin for their Sovereign and his Consort'.

Models of some Canadian wildlife, including deer and moose.

Bison and wolves were more examples of the fauna of the Dominion.

CANADIAN PAVILION.

Examples of Canadian minerals and resources on display.

The King spoke briefly, and to the point:

> Gentlemen, I thank you for your loyal and cordial welcome. I regretted my inability to be present for the opening ceremony of the Exhibition, and it is with real pleasure that the Queen and I, without daughter, came here to-day to see for ourselves the results of your foresight, energy and patriotic effort … I heartily congratulate you upon the self-reliance and enterprise, of which the Exhibition, with its attractive surroundings is such a striking monument … I rejoice to learn from you that you are satisfied with the measure of success that has been already achieved, and I confidently hope that the final result may realise your fullest expectations … I shall, indeed, be glad if our visit tends in any way to secure this end, and to help in promoting the commercial and industrial prosperity of Ireland.

The royals then ate lunch (with 190 others) in the Palace Restaurant, with the daily newspapers printing the precise order, working away from the monarch, in which the fifty top table guests were seated. These consisted almost entirely of members of the Royal Party and the Irish aristocracy. Besides the Chief Secretary Augustine Birrell and his wife, the only commoners were Mr and Mrs A. Jameson, Mr W.M. Murphy and Miss Murphy, Mr and Mrs Talbot-Power and Mr and Mrs James Shanks.

After lunch they met another large throng, comprising the committees of the exhibition and other lesser notables. They then spent a short time visiting the exhibits, taking a particular diplomatic interest in the French, Italian and New Zealand sections, before enjoying a short programme of music assembled by Barton M'Guckin. The 300-strong choir sang the specially-composed *Come Back to Erin* by Sir Francis Brady, which was a gushing and toadying tribute to the royal couple which included the verse:

The French Pavilion, also visited by the King in a nod to the *Entente Cordiale*. It was opened by the Viceroy on 29 June as part of a deliberate policy of phased openings to keep up the public interest in the event.

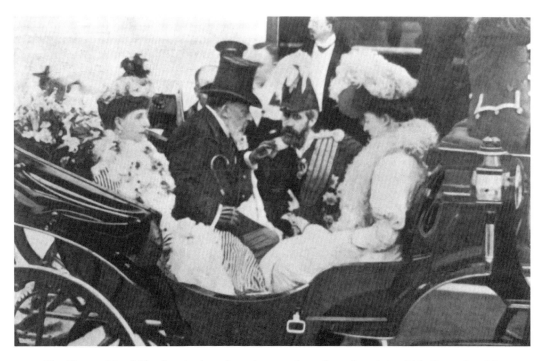

The King and Lord Aberdeen in deep discussion – perhaps about the missing Irish Crown jewels? – as the party leave the showgrounds.

These photographs were taken by an unknown photographer on a day trip to the exhibition. The photographs show the buildings from quirky angles, including a rare view of the Morehampton Road entrance. The final two pictures show Morehampton Road thronged with crowds as the viceregal carriage passes by. These photographs appear to have been taken from what is now Sachs Hotel.

> Come back to Erin, our Queen Alexandra!
> Never forgot be her goodness and love!
> Happy and long may her reign and her day be!
> Grateful and loyal all Ireland will prove!

The royals then took to their carriages once again. They received a tribute from the Somali villagers, who were 'clad in spotless white robes, and carried shining spears. Their chief led them in their singing of a hymnal air, to which the Royal party listened and smilingly acknowledged the kindly greeting.' They also visited the Home Industries section, where Lady Aberdeen gave them a guided tour and the King was presented with a case of pipes and the Queen a parasol from the Presentation Convent, Cork.

It wasn't all collecting gifts for the King, however. He took a fancy to a 'magnificent piece of pictorial enamel' entitled *A Falling Star* by P. Oswald Reeves, but when he asked to buy it was told that Lady Dudley had already purchased it. He then bought an enamelled coin box made by Miss Mary Doran of the Dublin Metropolitan School of Art. The royal party moved on to the Palace of Fine Arts where Alfred Temple conducted them around. The royals showed a special interest in the collection of Irish historical relics collected by Colonel Courteney. After a quick visit to the Canadian Pavilion, the party left the exhibition at 4.15 p.m., fifteen minutes later than scheduled, before leaving the exhibition through the Morehampton Road gate.

The cortège were greeted by enthusiastic crowds that thronged the streets from Donnybrook to the city centre. At the junction where Grafton Street meets Nassau Street and Suffolk

Street, a large crown was suspended over the road, from which arches of flowers reached to the buildings on the corners. The whole effect was of the parade passing under a floral canopy. The parade carried up Sackville (now O'Connell) Street and into Rutland (now Parnell) Square, before travelling along North Frederick Street, Berkeley Road and North Circular Road before entering the Phoenix Park.

At a garden party in the lodge, they then had to receive eleven more loyal addresses from organisations such as the Royal Dublin Society, the Royal Zoological Society, the Dublin Chamber of Commerce and the Apothecaries' Hall. It has been surmised that the reason there were so many tributes was to disguise the fact that there was no official welcome from the Corporation of Dublin. Another notable absentee was Sir Arthur Vicars who had handed out the badges of the Knights of St Patrick at the exhibition's opening ceremony, but on whose watch the Irish Crown jewels had been stolen in the interim.

At six o'clock the royals returned to the yacht by motor car and the King spent the next day at the Leopardstown races. It is not recorded whether or not the King met a prominent racehorse owner/trainer who had his home and stables close to the course. Richard 'Boss' Croker was a notorious Irish-American politician who, on retiring from Tammany Hall, had bought a large house in south Dublin. From his stables at Glencairn (now the residence of the British Ambassador), Croker sent out the aforementioned Orby to win the Epsom Derby in June 1907. There were reports that the King left the royal box soon afterwards to avoid having to meet the controversial winning owner, which tradition dictated he should have done. Croker's win was warmly celebrated in Dublin, with an old woman famously remarking to Orby's owner, 'Thank God and you, Sir, that we have lived to see a Catholic horse win the English Derby.'

The King clearly enjoyed his day at Leopardstown, as he was too exhausted to bother waving to the Dubliners on his return to the Phoenix Park. For most of the journey in the royal landau he was fast asleep.

The Palace of Industries and the left wing of the domed palace. The attendance often exceeded 20,000 people a day.

six

Exhibition within an Exhibition

The weather in 1907 was not particularly good, and the organisers were relieved that they had so many indoor attractions. An *Irish Times* writer on June 3 commented that 'there had been rain that day, but in the intervals of sunshine the ladies burst forth in all the glory of their dainty summer toilettes!' The following month was no better, when a reporter wrote that 'the unpleasant weather which we are resiled has had the effect of rendering the grounds of the Exhibition a scene of vernal luxuriance'.

Because of the increasing interest, a decision was taken to open the exhibition on Sundays, which drew the wrath of Sabbatarians. Revd E.H. Lewis-Crosby, rector of Drumcondra and North Strand, wrote to *The Irish Times* to complain that 'the one day of the week which the workers have should not be unnecessarily filched from them'.

The event continued to draw distinguished visitors from all over the world. On 12 July it was visited by Georg Hackenschmidt, undisputed wrestling champion of the world, who was performing at the Theatre Royal. 'The Russian Lion' is remembered as the inventor of 'The Bear Hug'.

Special editions of several publications were devoted to Dublin, including a three-part series of the *Art Magazine* and the May issue of the *World's Work*, which was designated 'The Irish Number'. This later journal featured a special article by Mr Bram Stoker on 'The Great White Fair in Dublin' and a piece on 'How Ireland Got A National Trade Mark' by John Pius Boland MP, the winner of the gold medal for tennis at the first modern Olympic Games in 1896.

Several other publications emerged from the exhibition itself. An eight or twelve-page programme was produced daily, detailing the special events of the day and the ever-changing line-up of bands and musical performers. A thirty-two-page booklet entitled the *Irish International Exhibition, 1907* was issued in 1906 to help drum up business and was sponsored by the White Star Line. Written by the Chairman of the Admission, Traffic and Publicity Committee, R.S. Tresilian, it contained drawings of the proposed buildings as well as photographs of Dublin scenes. It set out the planned exhibits and attractions, as well as those of the city as a whole. An updated edition was produced in 1907 to act as a guide.

Richard Tresilian was born in Bandon, Co. Cork and was in his twenties when he was appointed Secretary and Manager of the North Dublin Street Tramways Company on its foundation in 1875. In 1881 the tramways companies were amalgamated and Tresilian was employed as Assistant Secretary to the Dublin Tramways Company. A further amalgamation occurred in 1896 when the Dublin United Tramways Company absorbed some other concerns and Tresilian was appointed secretary. He held this role until his death in May 1915. Tresilian's obituary said he was 'keenly interested in statistical problems, and was an able organiser'. He would get plenty of opportunity to show his talents as the exhibition came together.

In 1909 a large, bound report was produced; *Record: The Irish International Exhibition 1907*, compiled and edited by William F. Dennehy. A large and ornate volume, it printed no less than sixty-six portraits of the exhibition's bigwigs on its 344 pages. There was also the *Handbook of Irish Rural Life and Industry*.

Public health, or rather the poor state of it, had begun to interest people through the efforts of the Womens' Health Institute of Ireland which published a magazine called *Slainte*, meaning 'health'. One two-storey building at the exhibition was used to demonstrate baby incubators which were, as its advertising screamed outside, 'containing live babies!'

The viceregal couple, Lord and Lady Aberdeen.

Above: Examples of isolation shelters for those suffering from tuberculosis were on display at the exhibition in the closing weeks.

Left: Richard Tresilian, Chairman of the Admissions, Traffic and Publicity Committee.

Above, left and right: Front and back of the committee medal issued to Tresilian. This was purchased in 2005 from an eBay seller in New Zealand.

Right: The world champion wrestler Georg Hackenschmidt visited the exhibition in July.

Above and below: Photographs were hand-coloured to produce attractive postcards, and occasionally the artist took great licence. The people in these pictures are in exactly the same positions and poses, although one appears to have been taken at night.

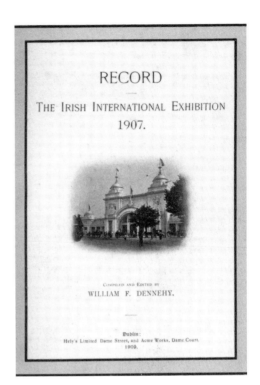

Frontispiece of the monumental official *Record of the Irish Industrial Exhibition of 1907*, which was published two years later.

Another of the exhibition's publishing ventures, written by committee member William McCarthy-Filgate.

A competition was held to design cottages for labourers.

For three weeks towards the end of the run, the Countess of Aberdeen established a special 'exhibition within an exhibition' in the Home Industries section. She assembled a committee of many of the most eminent medical men and women of the day and special anti-tuberculosis displays and lectures were staged. It was quite a shocking exhibit, with diseased lungs on show in large jars and photographs of sputum enlarged 5,000 times. There were on show specimens of chalets where stricken family members could be isolated in back gardens.

One of the outstanding public figures of her time, Lady Aberdeen was born Ishbel Marjoribanks in 1857, the daughter of the first Baron Tweedsmouth, and married the first Marquess of Aberdeen in 1877. He became Governor-General of Canada in 1893 and remained in that office for the next five years. While in Canada she threw herself into campaigns against tuberculosis and for the rights of women. She was President of the International Council of Women for nearly forty years, from 1893 until 1899 and 1904 to 1936. She died in Scotland in 1939.

She showed similar energies in her public work in Ireland. She organised playgrounds for children in the inner-city slum areas, and set up a milk run to provide nutrition to impoverished children. She founded the Women's National Health Association, which in 1912 opened the Peamount Sanatorium in Newcastle, Co. Dublin. She had an unstuffy approach to socialising, and introduced afternoon receptions where members of the community would 'drop in, meet their friends and have a cup of tea'; a far cry from the grand balls of their predecessors. One of the balls she did hold in 1907, the Irish Lace Ball, was again part of her campaign to promote Irish home industry, as all those attending were required to dress in Irish lace. She had caused a social scandal while in Canada when she joined her servants to take high tea.

Lady Aberdeen had a particular passion for the fight against tuberculosis as four members of her husband's family had succumbed to the deadly disease. At the time her work in the field

This example of a traditional Irish cottage was also built in the grounds.

was denigrated by some nationalists; a sneering poem called 'The Ringsend Babies Club' was published with references to 'Mrs Microbe'. However it is certain she saved many Irish lives through her campaign for clean milk. The campaign against the scourge continued after the exhibition closed, with two travelling shows touring the country taking the message to the towns and villages. The Gaelic League co-operated with this venture and translated the display boards and organised lectures in Irish.

Tuberculosis, colloquially known as TB, was a devastating killer in all sectors of Irish society. In 1907 11,679 people died; 15 per cent of all deaths that year and 2.7 per 1,000 of the population of the country. Lady Aberdeen was determined to fight the disease and selected the exhibition as the starting point for a wide public campaign. Early in 1907 she decided to form a Women's National Health Association and acted quickly to do so. Her husband inaugurated the association at a public meeting in the Royal College of Physicians in March 1907, where its aims were announced: to arouse public opinion, and particularly that of the women of Ireland, to a sense of responsibility regarding the public health; to spread the knowledge of what may be done in every home and by every householder to guard against disease and to eradicate it when it appears; to promote the upbringing of a healthy and vigorous race.

The Tuberculosis Exhibition was held in the village hall and in the Industrial Hall of the Irish Industries section. The exhibits were divided into four parts—the Statistical, Literary, Pathological and Appliances, in which 'many exhibits of an instructive and convincing character were shown'. The Lord Lieutenant himself opened the exhibition on 12 October, when a message of support from the King was read out. Almost every day for the rest of the exhibition a lecture was delivered by a leading expert, as well as demonstrations of 'invalid cookery' and the pasteurisation and sterilisation of milk. Attendance at these was enormous, several being

The volunteer fire brigade had thankfully few blazes to deal with.

over-subscribed. On 7 November a conference on district nursing was held and the following day the Tuberculosis Exhibition closed with a special lecture on 'the Control of Milk and Food Supplies'. The official report of the exhibition, published in 1909, asserted that 'the latest statistics collected by the Registrar-General show that this effort has already produced salutary results'. Sir Robert Matheson's *A Review of the Anti-Tuberculosis Campaign in Ireland* praised the impact of the exhibition, noting that it had helped in the 'decrease of the habit [of] spitting'. Nevertheless, it was to be the middle of the twentieth century before medical advances really began to win the battle against the disease in Ireland.

The organisation of the show ran smoothly throughout its six months duration. There was concern at an early stage that the wooden structures that housed the exhibition would be easy prey to fire, whether started maliciously or accidentally. An elaborate system of high-pressure water mains was laid down around the grounds, with hydrants at short intervals between the buildings. Although the Pembroke Urban District Council had its own fire brigade, it was deemed necessary to organise an Exhibition Volunteer Fire Brigade composed of officials and workers on the exhibition. Edward Martin Murphy, son of William, headed up this grouping and spent a great amount of time organising and drilling the corps.

The exhibition report praised his efforts, stating that 'the Brigade was as fully equipped in every respect as that of any municipality, and proved its efficiency in combating several serious fires which occurred within the precincts of the Exhibition'. This was an exaggeration, as Murphy's own report said there were no serious fires, although there was a number of minor ones. On each night there was a firework display, a number of men were stationed on the roof of the art gallery in case of falling sparks. They were not needed although a spent rocket did crash through the glass roof of the gallery. Murphy's report also exhorted the committee to seek a rebate from the insurance companies: 'We understand that these companies charged exceedingly high rates, and the absence of a serious fire was entirely due to the efficiency and vigilance of a Private Brigade …'

Thomas Grant, a chief superintendent of the Dublin Metropolitan Police, was assigned to the exhibition for the duration and was happy to report that 'not a single untoward incident arose within the Exhibition or its environs'. Around 25 sergeants and 250 constables were assigned duty every month to the exhibition. Although the police made no arrests, at the beginning of the run three English pickpockets had been arrested outside the grounds by D.J. Jauncey of the Manchester City Police, and a George Thompson was sentenced to three months in jail, while there was also some vandalism reported once the exhibition had closed. In another unfortunate incident, Inspector Mark Foran was injured when he was knocked down by a bicycle and was then run over by a hackney.

Almost 1,000 people had been employed for the duration of the exhibition. At one stage before opening Humphreys had 1,600 men working on the buildings, although it averaged 400 per week. In all, Humphreys paid out £35,000 in wages. There were also 100 plasterers, 200 painters, 150 plumbers and over 100 carpenters employed. The electrical contractors, Wm Coates, employed fifty men for the duration of the exhibition, with as many as eighty men at one time.

The 938 directly employed by the organisers included 6 clerks, 27 ground staff, 65 turnstile operators and watchmen, 29 engineers, 37 cloak room and lavatory assistants, 74 carpenters and labourers, 42 firemen, 24 home industry workers, 51 side show attendants, 12 attendants in concert and cinema halls. To these 397 must be added 541 who worked on the catering department (44 clerks and chefs, 99 waiters and 398 general including waitresses). They were paid a total of £23,057 in wages and salaries.

seven

A Farewell Glance

The closing ceremony was held at 4 p.m. on Saturday 9 November in the Concert Hall in the presence once more of Lord and Lady Aberdeen. The pair arrived along Morehampton Road and drove up Royal Avenue to the Grand Central Palace. More than 2,000 people attended the obsequies, and a Berlioz march was played as the Aberdeens walked up the aisle to their golden chairs perched on a scarlet dais. The Marquess of Ormonde read an address to the throng, in which he announced that the attendance was 'nearly two million and three-quarters'. He declared the exhibition a huge success, as it induced 'large numbers to visit Ireland from Great Britain and abroad, especially from the United States of America'. He hoped that Irish manufacturers would take this opportunity and follow it up, 'and find even outside of Ireland, as well as in our country, an increasing demand for the work of Irish hands'. He also pointed to the economic benefits that fell upon the city, with enormous business for hotels, restaurants and transport companies among others, 'far exceeding, as the council have reason to believe, the whole expenditure on the Exhibition itself'.

Ormonde also highlighted the benefits 'conferred upon considerable numbers of working people, to whom well paid employment was afforded on the construction of the buildings and laying out of the grounds during a period of more than usual depression'. He revealed that the exhibition's outgoings on wages totalled in excess of £2,000 per week during the period it was open.

The viceroy spoke, without notes, and paid full praise to the organisers, but complained that:

> ... it is quite certain that if the weather had not been so unusually – you might say abnormally – unpropitious, the number of visitors would have been very much greater. However, no one will attach any responsibility to the management for that!

He ended with the motto of the city of Aberdeen, 'Happy to meet, Sorry to part, Hope to meet again.' He then declared the event closed.

Barton M'Guckin then took over with a spectacular and stirring musical programme to complete the closing ceremony, assisted by 800 performers. *Rakoczy March* by Berlioz was followed by 'Hail, Bright Abode' from Wagner's *Tannhäuser*; *Die Meistersinger*, also by Wagner; and a fanfare of trumpets composed for the occasion. The programme was completed by the chorus from *Lobgesang* by Mendelssohn, 'Let Erin Remember' by Thomas Moore, the overture from *Tannhäuser* and the *Hallelujah Chorus* by Handel. The finale consisted of the Irish anthem *St Patrick's Day* and *God Save the King*.

With that, the Aberdeens bade farewell, climbed aboard their carriage and took off into the night. Entertainment was provided that last evening and 20,000 people packed the grounds to sample the atmosphere. The *Irish Independent* reporter wrote:

> The idea uppermost in the minds of all was that of taking a farewell glance at scenes which to nearly all had become familiar within the past six months … It was no wonder then to find the Industrial and Machinery Hall and other centres of attraction in the Exhibition crowded by visitors, many of whom purchased souvenirs of the great event.

The pavilion advertised on the walls outside that their products were demonstrated 'With Live Infants'.

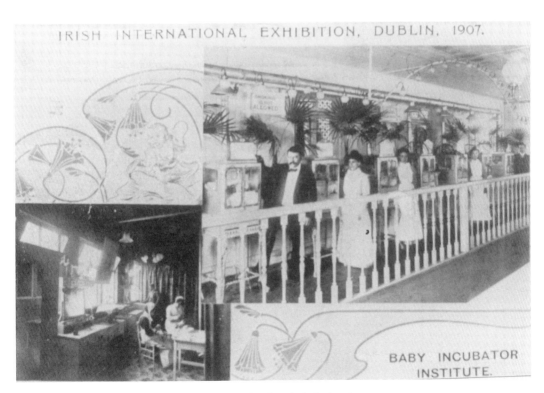

Ladies and gentlemen examine the latest technology in baby incubators.

The sideshows, too, came in for an extensive patronage:

> When the visitors had 'done the rounds', and satisfied themselves that they had taken their parting look of the grounds, they literally swarmed into the Central Hall and into the Concert Hall. In the former place Ireland's Own Band performed a selection of music both in the afternoon and evening, while at the conclusion of the Official Closing Ceremony Herr Kandt's band played an attractive farewell programme, in which were included some of those delightfully catchy items so popular with the afternoon audiences for the last month. 'Standing room only' was the order during this performance, which wound up with a fine rendering of the 'Ireland Ever' finale. Following on the termination of the Kandt programme came the magnificent performance of the Coldstream Guards, under Lieut Mackenzie-Rogan, who brought his audience – packed to the doors and on to the platform – to a high pitch of enthusiasm. Chief of the many splendid pieces performed was *1812* with organ effects. At its conclusion the band came in for a great ovation.

On that final evening the Executive Committee hosted a dinner for William Martin Murphy, at which he said he undertook the task of organising the exhibition 'solely through the realisation of the existence of urgent patriotic obligation, and with a view to overcoming an unreasoning opposition, which, if it could triumph, would prove fatal to the self-respect and prosperity of the people'.

When the dust finally settled and the final tallies were made, Murphy's exhibition took pride of place in the league table of previous Irish exhibitions.

Date	Venue	Area	Attendance
1850	(Kildare Street)	1 acre	300,000
1853	(Merrion Street)	2 acres	956,295
1865	(Earlsfort Terrace)	6 acres	724,958
1872	(Earlsfort Terrace)	6 acres	420,000
1882	(Rotunda Gardens)	3 acres	261,205
1907	(Herbert Park)	52 acres	2,751,113

Judged by the profit and loss account, the Great White Fair was a failure, though the official record went on to argue:

> In reality, however, there was not one of the business subscribers to the Guarantee Fund who did not benefit commercially and financially during the period the Exhibition remained open far in excess of the amount of liability incurred. Generous acknowledgement of this fact was publicly made by practically all the larger guarantors.

The Shelbourne Hotel, for example, took a record 49,671 guests over the year, with a single room costing 8s 6d per night and a double 15s.

The final accounts of the exhibition make interesting reading. They cover income and expenditure for the period from 10 July 1903 to 14 May 1909. Admissions took in £78,891, but the catering department took in an even larger sum of £80,284. The sideshows grossed £26,258 and other exhibits £22,886. A sum of £20,000 was realised when the buildings and plant were sold off after the closure of the exhibition. The total income was £340,313 16s 9½d. The estimated liabilities were just £1,100, coincidentally the precise sum, including costs, awarded against the exhibition after a legal battle with the Pembroke council.

A selection of the many amusing and risqué postcards produced for sale at the exhibition. Many designs were adapted slightly and resold at other exhibitions in Britain.

In full swing
at the Exhibition

THE EXHIBITION.
"Considerable interest is manifested by the visitors in the Brewing and Distilling Section."
Policeman — "Now, can't ye's take it quiet, sure there's enough in there to give a whole
gineration of ye the delairiums!"

The last tram from the Exhibition.

"It's no good you going up, mum, you'd stick!"

WHAT HO! SHE BUMPS.

Irish International Exhibition, Dublin, 1907.

Grand Concert Hall.

PROGRAMME OF

MUSICAL PERFORMANCE

ON THE OCCASION OF

The Closing of the Exhibition, November 9th, 1907.

The Band & Chorus will comprise 800 Performers.

Musical Director:

Mr. BARTON McGUCKIN.

Leader   Mr. PATRICK DELANEY.

The Orchestra will be composed of a number of well-known Dublin Musicians, and Members of H. M. Coldstream Guards, Herr Kandt's, and the Grandpierre Bands.

Official Organist   Mr. BRENDAN J. ROGERS.

The musical programme for the closing ceremony on Saturday 9 November 1907.

Opposite above: With the water chute dismantled and the exhibition a memory, Herbert Park opened to the public in 1911. A tiny bandstand was erected where the chute once stood.

Opposite below: The bustling crowds are gone and Herbert Park settles into its future as a splendid suburban amenity.

While the total published number of visitors topped 2¾ millions, the breakdown of admission tickets show that 1,115,664 people paid the full admission of one shilling, and a further 245,878, such as children, paid smaller sums. Almost 14,000 people bought season tickets at prices up to one guinea.

The details of each of the sideshows were published, showing the varying deals done with the providers. The hobby horse and swingboats entrepreneur, Mr Toft, had to pay 50 per cent of receipts, leaving little more than £700 for himself. The most popular exhibit of all was the Somali Village, which took £9,601, of which 25 per cent (£2,400) was handed over to the exhibition. The promoter of the Baby Incubator also struck a handsome deal, agreeing a fixed sum of £250 which was a tiny proportion of his receipts of £2,412. Some other exhibits were the property of the exhibition and thus yielded the full receipts. The highly popular water chute took in £7,094 and the switchback railway £4,505.

The cost of the erection of the buildings came to £118,061, and the lavatories and plumbing £3,563. The laying down of the roads and paths cost £17,106 and drains cost £3,660. The bandstand, which lay at the far end of the pond to the current, far less imposing one, cost £521 to erect.

The exhibition spawned a mini-industry of souvenirs and mementos. Many items such as these can still be bought for small sums today.

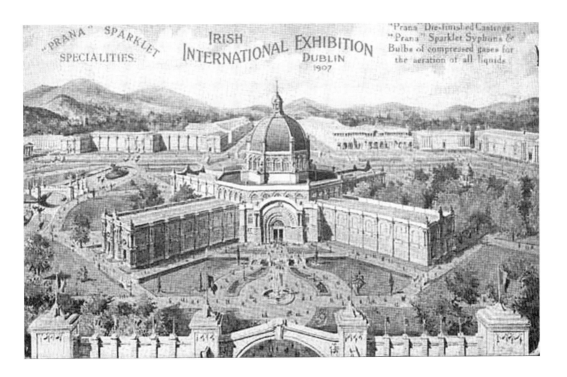

Although the exhibition had closed, there were still more than fifty committee meetings held thereafter. The buildings and materials were sold off piecemeal over the next eighteen months but the main problem that arose was a demand for £11,000 from the Pembroke Township Council. The exhibition was obliged to vacate the site on 29 June 1908, but had not completed their work by that date. William Martin Murphy asked for two or three weeks more to complete their work and promised to 'hire a large number of men to expedite the clearance, and, as far as possible, to put the grounds into a reasonable condition'. The problem was that the contract stipulated that if the exhibition were still occupying the grounds it would be liable for an extra £1,000 rent. Murphy offered to retain the workmen to clean up the grounds but would not pay any extra rent. The council turned down the offer and the workers withdrew.

The exhibition then offered £1,000 as a full settlement but the Pembroke Township Council rejected this and the matter went to court. The local authority won there, but was awarded just £500, which did not even cover its own legal costs. The exhibition had a similar bill to pay.

A meeting to wind-up the financial affairs of the committee was held on 20 May 1909 in the offices of Casey, Clay and Collins Solicitors and present were W.M. Murphy, Col. Courtney, R.S. Tresilian, W.F. Dennehy and another twenty members of the Executive Committee. Murphy told the meeting that the liability for each member who guaranteed £50 was just £1. The very last act of the company was the meeting of creditors in the Central Hall, Westmoreland Street, on 4 June 1909. The guarantors had to pay a sum close to £100,000 but the benefit to the city and the country was far in excess of that. Murphy also told the meeting that he could not give an 'absolutely final statement', because of the pending question of costs in relation to the Pembroke council's legal action. Murphy said that the action was forced on the company, 'we did not allow it to go on without making efforts to settle it, and that we thought we would be doing what was fair to the council and saving the Association money by offering £1,000'.

Eventually the grounds were enclosed again and railings erected around the thirty-two acre Herbert Park and the road through it opened to the public. It was handed over by the Earl of Pembroke to the Pembroke Urban District Council in 1911 (although a sign at the park today says it was established in 1903). In 1932 the park was handed over to Dublin Corporation whose Parks Department manages it today. The only visible reminder of the Great White Fair is the pond, still popular with walkers and duck-feeders, although its original *raison d'etre* is long gone. Herbert Park is a popular amenity in a busy and prosperous area, but even still it is hard to imagine the hustle and bustle of those three million visitors, during those magical six months, a century ago.